高校学术研究论著丛刊
人文社科

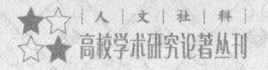

英语阅读教学理论
与经典研读实践研究

廖 肖 著

中国书籍出版社
China Book Press

图书在版编目(CIP)数据

英语阅读教学理论与经典研读实践研究 / 廖肖著
. -- 北京：中国书籍出版社，2022.8
ISBN 978-7-5068-9152-3

Ⅰ.①英… Ⅱ.①廖… Ⅲ.①英语-阅读教学-教学研究 Ⅳ.①H319.37

中国版本图书馆 CIP 数据核字(2022)第 157283 号

英语阅读教学理论与经典研读实践研究

廖 肖 著

策划编辑	谭 鹏 武 斌
责任编辑	马丽雅
责任印制	孙马飞 马 芝
封面设计	东方美迪
出版发行	中国书籍出版社
地 址	北京市丰台区三路居路 97 号(邮编：100073)
电 话	(010)52257143(总编室) (010)52257140(发行部)
电子邮箱	eo@chinabp.com.cn
经 销	全国新华书店
印 厂	三河市德贤弘印务有限公司
开 本	710 毫米×1000 毫米 1/16
字 数	182 千字
印 张	11.5
版 次	2023 年 3 月第 1 版
印 次	2023 年 9 月第 2 次印刷
书 号	ISBN 978-7-5068-9152-3
定 价	80.00 元

版权所有 翻印必究

目 录

第一章　绪论 ……………………………………………………………… 1
　　第一节　英语阅读的定义与分类 …………………………………… 1
　　第二节　阅读过程与注意力 ………………………………………… 5
　　第三节　眼动阅读指标 ……………………………………………… 12
　　第四节　阅读能力的本质 …………………………………………… 19

第二章　英语阅读与英语语言知识 …………………………………… 23
　　第一节　英语阅读与词汇知识 ……………………………………… 23
　　第二节　英语阅读与句法知识 ……………………………………… 36
　　第三节　英语阅读与篇章知识 ……………………………………… 42

第三章　英语阅读教学设计概述 ……………………………………… 46
　　第一节　英语阅读教学活动设计的必要性 ………………………… 46
　　第二节　英语阅读准备活动设计 …………………………………… 48
　　第三节　英语知识与领会活动设计 ………………………………… 54
　　第四节　英语阅读分析与评价活动设计 …………………………… 69

第四章　英语阅读教学之学习策略探索 ……………………………… 78
　　第一节　英语阅读策略分析 ………………………………………… 78
　　第二节　英语阅读策略之逻辑关系 ………………………………… 82
　　第三节　英语阅读策略之略读 ……………………………………… 87
　　第四节　英语阅读策略之篇章结构 ………………………………… 91
　　第五节　英语阅读中的其他策略 …………………………………… 103

第五章　英语阅读教学中的方法掌握探索 …………………… 107
　第一节　阅读方法简述 …………………………………… 107
　第二节　影响阅读效果的要素 …………………………… 120
　第三节　阅读技能的训练 ………………………………… 129
　第四节　英语阅读中应处理好的几个关系 ……………… 131

第六章　英语阅读教学经典研读实践探索 …………………… 134
　第一节　示范性阅读与解析 ……………………………… 134
　第二节　经典美文阅读与解析 …………………………… 142
　第三节　名言警句阅读与欣赏 …………………………… 163
　第四节　独立阅读实践训练 ……………………………… 164

参考文献 …………………………………………………………… 172

第一章 绪 论

阅读是人们获取知识的重要途径之一。在英语学习过程中,每个人都要不断提高自己的阅读技能。本章作为全书开篇,首先对英语阅读的相关基础知识展开分析,为下文的展开做好铺垫。

第一节 英语阅读的定义与分类

一、英语阅读的定义

说起英语阅读,似乎无人不知,无人不晓。大部分人对英语阅读的定义就是通过眼睛的扫视、移动在以英语为语言媒介的书籍、印刷物、电子出版物以及互联网等媒体上获取信息、知识的过程。

在《牛津现代高级英汉双解辞典》(1984)中,我们可以发现有多达 9 种对单词 read 的解释,其一为:look at and be able to understand something written or printed,即指看并能理解某些书面或印刷的东西,读,看懂;其二为:reproduce mentally or vocally the words of an author, book, ect.,即通过头脑或口头再现某个作者、图书等的语句,亦即阅读、默读、朗诵;其三为:study a subject, especially at a university,即指研究、攻读一门学科,尤其指在大学中研读;其四为:interpret mentally, learn the significance of,即解释、解答、领会……的意义;其五为:give a certain impression; seem (good etc.) when read,即给予某种印象,读起来似乎是……;其六为:assume, find implications in what is read, etc.,即假

定或找出所读之物等中的含意；其七为：(of instruments) indicate，即指仪器显示；其八为：bring into a specified state by reading，即指由阅读而进入某种状态；其九为：having knowledge gained from books, etc.，即有从书中得来知识的，有书本知识的。①

在非节略本的《兰登英语大词典》（第2版，1987）中，对单词 read 的解释竟多达35种，其中23种将其用作及物动词，12种用作不及物动词。除了与《牛津现代高级英汉双解词典》中的一些解释相似的以外，《兰登英语大词典》中还做了大量的补充。例如：

(1) to apprehend the meaning of signs, characters, ect., otherwise than with the eyes, as by means of the fingers，即通过用眼睛以外的其他方式如用手来理解一些诸如符号、标志及字符等含义；(2) to apprehend or interpret the meaning of gestures, movements, signals, or the like，即明白或了解手势、动作、信号等诸如此类的东西；(3) to have such knowledge of a language as to be able to understand things written in it，即拥有相关的语言知识，能理解用此语言所写的东西；(4) to infer something not expressed or directly indicated from what is read, considered, or observed，即推断、推理；(5) to check printers' proofs, copy, etc. for errors; proofread，即校读、校对。其他的一些解释我们在这里不再一一赘述。

在 Teaching Reading Skills in a Foreign Language（《外语阅读技巧教学》，1983）这本书中，作者 Christine Nuttall（纳托尔）指出，人们对阅读的定义各不相同，但是大家通常会用到这样三组英语词汇：(1) understand, interpret, meaning, sense, etc.；(2) decode, decipher, identify, etc.；(3) articulate, speak, pronounce, etc.。

综合以上人们对阅读的不同解释，我们可以将英语阅读比较全面地定义为：信息接受者或信息发出者通过利用各种感知觉器官（眼、耳、口、手等）对英语语言以及与其相关的图形、文字、信号、标志、声音等进行感知、理解、分析、归纳、总结、评判以及推断等的过程。

二、英语阅读的分类

英语阅读的分类比较多元化。我们可以根据英语阅读的定义中所

---

① 韩满玲，邓保中.英语阅读的奥秘[M].北京：中国国际广播出版社，2006.

第一章 绪 论

涉及的各个方面将英语阅读按以下情况加以区分。

按阅读所利用的感知觉器官来分,我们认为有以下几种。

(1)朗读:即主要通过口头表述来感知、获取、理解和表达英语语言文字及相关的信息的阅读形式。

(2)听读:即主要通过听觉来感知、获取和理解信息的形式。听读对一些人来说可能比较生疏,但是对于那些不能通过视觉看书报、屏幕等可显示文字信息和其他视觉符号、标识,而必须通过听力来获取和解读世界的人来说,其所用的阅读方式应该说就是听读了,如听父母朗读故事的婴幼儿、听收音机广播或磁带等语音材料扩展知识的盲人或其他普通人。

(3)默读:即主要通过视觉(眼睛)来感知、获取、解读信息的方式,而读者在做这种阅读时嘴巴不发声,只是心理认知和解读所看到的文字及其他相关材料。

(4)触读:即主要通过手、脚、口、皮肤等触觉器官感知、获取和理解所接触或触摸到的文字、符号、标识、图形等的方式,如盲人在阅读盲文时即采用这种阅读方式。

按阅读所利用的时间多少来划分,则可以将阅读分为:

(1)快速阅读:即阅读速度较一般逐词逐句阅读的速度要快许多,通常阅读的速度可以达到每分钟500至1000个英语单词,主要用于了解所读材料的主题大意、特定细节等。

(2)中速阅读:即以一般的阅读速度来处理所读材料中的字词,几乎是逐词逐句阅读,通常阅读的速度是每分钟200至300个左右英语单词,主要用于了解所读材料的大部分信息和细节。

(3)慢速阅读:即以比一般中速阅读速度还要慢的速度来处理所读文字、词句、图表等,不仅要逐词逐句阅读大部分内容,而且某些重要部分或疑难部分还需要反复阅读才能理解,通常阅读的速度要低于每分钟200个英语单词,主要用于解难答疑、深入研究和评判推断等。

按阅读的目的来划分,则可以将阅读分为:

(1)精读:阅读的目的是详细了解所读材料中的各种信息和内容,从深度上挖掘文章寓意。

(2)泛读:即阅读的目的是扩大自己的知识面,在解读所读材料的深度和准确度上不做很高的要求,只需要对所读材料有一个大体的了解。在阅读的广度上有比较高的要求,同时泛读也与阅读速度有直接的相关性。泛读的主要目的是博览群书,广泛拓展知识面,阅读各种文字材料,提高英语词汇量和对文章的一般解读能力。

(3)校读:即阅读的目的是检验所读的材料中是否有语言、内容、版面、体例等方面的错误,这种阅读通常报刊、图书的编辑和校对人员会用到,而在其他场合、实际生活、工作和学习中我们也时时会采用。如学习中写完某些论文或文章、作业等的校读,工作中报告、文件、文书在正式上呈或下发前的校读等。在进行校读时,人们对语言和内容的准确性要求最高。

按阅读的方法来划分,我们可以将英语阅读分为以下几种。

(1)浏览式阅读:即在阅读文章时为了能够在比较短的时间内了解文章的主旨大意、全文要点信息等所采用的一种快速阅读方法,其主要特点是只阅读书籍的各个章节目录、文章的主标题、副标题,文章中的黑体字部分,文章的第一自然段和最后一个自然段即首尾段落以及每个段落的第一句和最后一句即首尾句,通过阅读这些内容就可以比较迅速地大概了解书籍和文章的主要内容和主题等要点信息。

(2)查阅式阅读:是指为了了解某些具体细节或解决某些特殊问题而进行的一种一目十行式的略读方式。这种阅读方法比较简便易行,类似于根据所给生词在词典中查找该生词词义的阅读方法,因此我们称之为查阅式阅读。这种阅读的目的性极强,阅读速度也非常快,适用于阅读各种英语文字材料,并且在英语阅读理解测试中也是常见的、有效的、必用的阅读方法。

(3)跳跃式阅读:是指在阅读材料时,为了加快阅读速度、提高阅读效率、抓住重点信息而根据文章的写作方式、组织结构和句子的语法结构、语言安排以及标点符号的提示而采用的快速阅读方式。利用这种跳跃式阅读法既可以提高阅读速度,又可以在有限的时间里掌握文章的主要内容和关键细节等,是一种值得推广的当代英语阅读方法。

(4)意群式阅读:即在阅读材料时利用视幅的变化将文字中的每个词句读到眼睛里,反映到头脑中,在处理每个词句时不是孤立地一个一个词来阅读,而是根据句子结构、语法成分以及短语搭配等将句子的词语一组一组地映入眼帘,读通读懂整个句子的每一部分。这种阅读方法可以不省略任何信息,同时提高阅读速度和理解能力,我们在处理大多数文字材料时都习惯采用这种英语阅读方式。

(5)研究式阅读:是指在阅读文章、书籍的过程中,因为所读材料内容的生疏、艰涩,句子结构的复杂、冗长和词语丰富多变而引起阅读困难时人们常用的一种慢速阅读方法。研究式阅读的主要目的是要准确理解文章内容和词语含义,从而进行正确的引申推断和分析评判。因此,在进行研究式阅读时,人们通常要对有疑问和困难的部分仔细阅读几遍,反复思考,甚至需要翻译成母语才可以全面准确理解。用英语学习与专业相关的材料和内容时,人们常常要用到研究式阅读。

(6)欣赏式阅读:即在阅读一些文学作品时,读者对文章中感触颇深、震动较大之处进行的分析和赏析性阅读,可以通过大声朗读来欣赏文字的韵律美、词语美,也可以通过仔细分析和评判作品或其中某些部分给读者带来的人生启迪、社会意义、写作风格、修辞手法等方面来深入体会所读材料的无穷意味,欣赏式阅读主要用于文学作品的欣赏,有时也可以用作学习地道而又独特的英语写作时的辅助阅读。

第二节　阅读过程与注意力

一、阅读步骤

阅读是从书面语言中获取信息,进而加工编码,获得知识意义的活动过程;通常而言,阅读的过程可以分为七个步骤。这七个步骤是为了便于理解而加以划分的,它们之间多次交互反复,没有明显的先后之分。

(1)识别。认识字母符号,脑的作用和眼的作用不能分开。

(2)吸收。以单词为单位,光线进行反射,经过眼睛和视神经,最后传输到大脑。

(3)内部融合。即通常所讲的理解,这一步涉及句法信息、语用信息、文体等知识的调用。其中,句法信息对于大学生理解英语句子来讲至关重要。

(4)外部融合。以所读的内容为对象和刺激信号,激活以前掌握的知识,尤其是与阅读主题相关的背景,将两者联系起来进行思考,如分析、批判、选择、鉴赏、扬弃等。

(5)保留。信息的基本储存。为了应对考试,学生会储存所需的大量信息。显而易见,这些临时的储存不够用,必须和回忆结合起来。

(6)回忆。为了理解原文,在需要的时候对储存的信息加以检索,并进行信息反馈。

(7)交流。将信息立即或最终应用于交流的过程,这些应用包括写作、演讲、做题和其他的一些具有创造性的表达方式。

二、主要阅读方法

英语阅读能力的提高有两个重要标志:阅读速度加快,理解率提高。这两者应该平衡发展,共同提高。阅读方法直接影响着阅读的速度和质量,如果学生能根据阅读的目的选择和掌握正确的阅读方法,对于提高英语阅读能力、改善阅读过程有着重要的意义。常用的英语阅读方式主要有以下几种。

(一)浏览式阅读

目的:在比较短的时间内了解文章的主旨大意、中心思想、全文要点等信息。

适用场景:测试中涉及中心思想、最佳标题一类的问题。

文章阅读要点:(1)标题和次标题;(2)每段的首尾句和主题句;(3)特殊标志词:表示转折关系的 but、yet、however,表示总结、归纳、得出结论、因果关系的 thus、so、therefore,这些标志词往往伴随着主题句出现。

浏览式阅读是一种为了解全文大意、寻找文章中心思想而采用的快速阅读方式,在回答文章的全文中心信息、最佳标题等题目时较为有效。这种阅读可以大幅提高阅读速度,并帮助学生迅速准确地掌握文章总体篇章结构和文中的主要信息和关键词句。

(二)查阅式阅读

目的:查找特殊信息或具体细节,或者解决某些特殊问题。

适用场景:在测试中涉及具体细节和特殊信息的问题。

文章阅读要点:(1)题干中涉及的关键提示词,如专有名词、数字、年代等;(2)关键提示词所在的句子或段落。

查阅式阅读是为了解决某个特殊问题,寻找具体事实或相关信息而进行的一种一目十行式的快速阅读方式。此方法比较简便易行,类似于根据所给生词在词典中查找词义的阅读方法,因此我们称之为查阅式阅读。①

(三)跳跃式阅读

目的:加快阅读速度,提高阅读效率,掌握文章的全貌和要点,略去不重要的词句。

适用场景:涉及文章主题和观点的问题。

文章阅读要点:抓住文章中的各个句子的主干成分,即表达重点信息的主语、谓语、宾语等成分。

跳跃式阅读旨在掌握文章的全貌和要点,而且又不需要将文章中的所有词句全部映入眼帘、读入脑海,因为文章中总有些词语、句子是起着次要的补充说明和修饰限定作用的,像这样的内容就可以在第一遍快速跳跃式阅读时略过不读。因此跳跃式阅读主要是抓住要点信息,略去次要无用的词句,迅速理解文章主旨和掌握文章全貌。

(四)意群式阅读

目的:不省略任何信息,准确、详细地理解文章含义,又可以提高阅读速度。

适用场景:句子较长,学生具有一定的语法知识。

文章阅读要点:根据语法知识,将句子划分为几个意群,如主语部分、谓语部分、宾语部分、从句以及作状语、定语的介词短语等阅读单位;然后具体理解各部分的内容。

意群式阅读既可以帮助学生了解详细的词语信息,又可以提高阅读

---

① 葛文庚.新课程背景下高中英语阅读教学策略的调整与优化研究[J].校园英语,2022(13):18-20.

速度,它跳出了逐字逐句停顿式的阅读方式,以句子中的语法成分为阅读单位,能够扩大学生的视幅,了解句子中的要点信息,避免了重复阅读。

(五)默读

读者处在倾向于"开口读出"的趋势之中,而没有朗读,尽量抑制发音。默读不是一种缓慢而单调乏味的过程。默读中碰到重要的单词或概念时,学生可以有意识地增大默读的"音量"(在内心把它们"喊出来"),这样可以使阅读信息中的某些字节凸显出来。默读过程主要是由眼睛和大脑参与,眼睛感知到文字符号,直接反映到大脑中,完成阅读的"形—意"过程,省去"形—音—意"加工过程中的声音环节,从而提高阅读速度,这也被称为"眼脑直映"法。[①]

(六)指读

用手指、钢笔等指着一个个词进行阅读。阅读时不发出声音,有些学生在指读时,一边看一边用笔指点勾画,利于增强辨识度。指读的优点是有利于保持注意力和焦点,但手指和手掌会妨碍眼睛的视线。解决办法是使用一个细长的引导物,提高阅读速度。

(七)回读

有意识地回到那些自认为遗漏和误解的单词、词组或段落上去。为了理解所读的材料,学生总是有意识地返回去重读。阅读时要尽量控制自己,做到读完了就能读懂,从而有效地避免回读。

(八)回跳

回跳是一种视觉痉挛,下意识地回到刚读过的单词或词组上。回跳与回读不同,回读是有意识地控制眼睛去回看某一特定部分,而回跳往往是无意识的。这两种现象会增加阅读时间,为了提高阅读速度,学生

---

① 孟留军. 大学英语阅读实训[M]. 合肥:安徽大学出版社,2018.

要注意自己的阅读节奏,有意识地控制自己眼球往前移动一次时所"覆盖"的单词数,减少回读和回跳。

(九)应试阅读

应试阅读是指学生阅读的目的是完成考试中的题目。为了顺利地做好阅读题,需要掌握一些策略和技巧。这些策略包括上面提到的阅读方法。特别需要说明的是应试阅读不同于跳跃式阅读,跳跃式阅读是应试阅读中的一种策略。学生在应试阅读时应先看题干,带着问题读文章,平时要严格训练阅读速度。要提高阅读速度,可从五个方面考虑:(1)克服不良的阅读习惯;(2)进行限时阅读训练,如 250 词的材料限定 5 分钟左右;(3)寻找主题句;(4)培养词义推断能力;(5)提高对长难句及常用句式的理解能力。

三、影响阅读注意力的因素

任何阅读方法都是在学生注意力集中的状态下才能更加有效。否则,就会事倍功半。阅读时注意力不集中,往往不是注意力本身变弱,而是"注意力指针"的指向转到了别处,学生在个人的意识流中增加对自身"注意力指针转向"的敏感度,达到一种高度的"自觉",会有利于调整"注意力指针"的转向,回到阅读任务中来。可以把注意力看作一匹野马,而学生就是骑师。在大多数情况下,野马以自己的方式朝着它喜欢的方向奔驰,而且随意变道,而作为一个专业的骑师(学生),就需要驾驭你的"注意力"之马,把它调教到适合你当前阅读任务的方向上来。描述注意力的一些术语,如表 1-1 所示。

表 1-1 描述注意力的相关术语

注意稳定性	通过主观努力,将注意力维持在具体对象上的能力,包括持续时间和专注程度。注意力的稳定性是注意在时间这一维度上的特征,稳定的注意力是阅读顺利进行的保障。
注意广度	在同一时间内一个人能够清楚地觉察或认识客体的数量,也叫注意范围。注意广度的扩大,有助于学生在同样的时间内输入更多的信息,提高阅读效率。

续表

注意选择	指学生集中感知资源,并指向一个特定的目标,或目标的某些方面,对其他刺激客体的注意力会暂时降低,从而增进注意力的指向性。从某种意义上说,"注意"一词本身具有选择性意义。它的合成形式仍常用于强调。
注意控制	在注意力维持和选择注意任务中,抵制与任务不相关干扰的能力,包括抵制本能反应、第一反应。如果"注意控制"做不好,学生就会经常分心、不专注,容易被周围事物干扰。这样的学生在性格上也容易冲动,自律性不够。
注意分配	将注意力分配到两个或多个不同的任务中,并良好地协调处理,例如边看边做笔记,边听边讲边做笔记等。注意的分配与转移是密切联系的。注意的转移,是学生能根据一定的目的,主动地把注意从一个对象转移到另一个对象上。为了顺利完成某项复杂的活动,注意中心在不同对象间的迅速往返转移,就构成了注意分配现象。

注意力不集中是造成英语阅读效率低下的主要原因,阅读时注意力不集中有许多原因,包括:词汇困难、阅读材料难以理解、不合适的阅读速度、不正确的情绪状态、缺乏准备、兴趣不够和动力不足。

(一)词汇困难

学生进行英语阅读,词汇是基本功,词汇积累非一朝一夕之功。遇到不认识或不熟悉的单词,注意力将逐渐分散。碰到不认识的单词时,别急于去查词典,可在其下面画一道线,然后继续向下读。通常,这一单词的意义会在读下文的过程中变得清晰起来。到短文全篇读完时,如果实在没有看懂难词的意思,再检索词典,一次查清楚所有的单词。

(二)阅读材料难以理解

学生出于某种需要去阅读,在自己的基础一时无法提高的前提下,只能旱地拔葱,硬着头皮去读。其中也有一些技巧可以减轻阅读困难,如阅读引导术、略读、跳读、段落结构知识和预读等,对材料进行"反复阅读"。预读是学生要像侦察兵那样在真正阅读之前先行一步,找出文章中的难词、重要信息、确定文章的主题,利用自己关于文章主题的现有知识,或者简单查阅与主题相关的信息,进行匹配,然后再正式地阅读。

(三)不合适的阅读速度

阅读速度和理解率是互相制约的,二者应适当保持平衡。理解率介于70%—80%,说明阅读速度适中;理解率低于70%,应适当放慢,如果高于90%,则表示读得过慢,应适当加快。当遇到一篇较难的材料时,慢慢读、仔细地读,只是阅读方式之一,不一定是最佳的阅读方式。因为读得过慢,单位时间内获取的信息就很少,材料看起来就高不可攀。当学生的自我效能感缺失到一定的程度时,最后就有可能导致放弃阅读。对于阅读较难的材料,不妨读得快一些,学生要学习快速和变速阅读,要将自己时间、精力的付出和目标需要、材料的难度做匹配,从而选择合适的阅读速度。

(四)不正确的情绪状态

阅读时,如果情绪不佳,学生就需要"整理"个人头脑中的思绪,让自己去调动精力来积极地思考将要阅读的主题。可行的一种方法是快速地用笔做两分钟的"思维导图",集中思想,产生强烈的阅读欲望。做思维导图有利于学生调整自己的状态,回到阅读任务上来,潜下心来阅读。

(五)缺乏准备

阅读过程是一场比拼意志力的战斗。要提前把笔、稿纸、眼镜、词典及其他必要的东西放在附近备用,以免不必要的分心。同时进行大脑预热,以便获得足够的动力,支撑学生完成阅读任务。

(六)兴趣不够

缺乏兴趣常常与其他的困难相伴,如冒出来的陌生词汇经常打断理解的进程;材料的难度远远超出了学生的现有理解水平,不是学生跳一跳,就能够得着;身边没有必要的辅助工具,导致学生必须在其他的事情上走得更远;其他的想法不时地冒出来,引起"注意力指针"的偏转。

意志力强的学生会有意识地抵制,并且能够成功地压抑与阅读过程无关的想法和诱惑,而且这种意志力是可以通过"刻意训练"来进一步培养强化的。兴趣的产生有多种方法。对文章中的某些信息点画思维导图,然后再一步步完善会有利于学生产生兴趣。

学生分析自己对材料的个人看法会引导兴趣的产生。不妨让自己扮演"苛刻的批评家"的角色,对自己在阅读中看懂的信息点进行评判,特别集中于文章中的那些不足之处。正如古人所言:"嫌货才是买货人"。嫌弃产品有问题的客户,往往是对产品有购买意向的人,客户发现产品与自身的利益发生了关系,才会提出对产品的异议。学生挑剔文章的过程,就是兴趣产生的过程,也是驱动自己把文章读懂、读通和读下去的过程。

(七)动力不足

学生可分析一下自己要读某份材料的原因,找到原因所在,并且得到了自己的高度认可,动力也相应地"水涨船高"。学生要不断强化阅读目标在心目中的重要性,时常问自己:"我在何处?我在干什么?现在是什么时间?阅读的进展情况是否已经比计划的进度晚了?如果晚了,晚了多少?"这有助于学生提高自身的动力水平和专注能力。

第三节 眼动阅读指标

人的嗅觉是有适应性的,如果在同一种气味的环境里待久了,便对该气味不敏感了,甚至是闻不到了。人眼是否也有这种特性呢?即看某个物体久了,就看不到该物体了?事实并非如此,眼睛在阅读的过程中会做一些较小而规则的"跳动"。这些"跳动"不同于"眨眼",人能够意识到"眨眼",但"跳动"有可能都意识不到,就像胃肠的蠕动那样。此处"眼睛跳动(眼跳)"的概念也不同于学生有意识地将目光注视点从一个单词移动到别的单词上的"移位"。

在阅读一行文字时,眼睛并不是持续地沿着一条线移动,而是由

第一章 绪 论

很短的、快速的运动(眼跳)和短暂停留(注视)相间隔而成。阅读就是眼睛"跳跃—注视—跳跃—注视"的持续,现在学者多数认为只有在注视期间,眼睛才能吸收信息,这些停顿用去了大部分时间。眼睛看到某一个区域时,如长的单词、短语、句子,总的注视时间＝单次注视时间(约250ms)＋眼跳时间＋单次注视时间(约250ms)＋眼跳时间＋眼跳一次。

有些学者利用眼动仪来研究阅读过程。如果学生掌握一些眼动仪测量时采用的眼动指标,就会对阅读过程有一个更加深入的了解,从而在阅读时也就会更加自觉地运用这些指标,调整阅读的速度。眼动仪的取样率一般是1000—2000赫兹(Hz),即1000—2000次/秒。1毫秒或0.5毫秒才取样一次。1赫兹＝1次/秒,即在单位时间内完成振动的次数,单位为赫兹。单次平均注视时间约250ms,1/4s＝250ms,即一秒大约跳4次。1秒(s)＝1000毫秒(ms)。

参照闫国利等人(2013)的文章《阅读研究中的主要眼动指标评述》,眼动指标可分为两大类:一类是与眼睛何时移动有关的时间维度的眼动指标,另一类是与眼睛移动位置有关的空间维度的眼动指标。具体分类如表1-2所示。

表1-2 阅读研究中的主要眼动指标

时间维度的眼动指标	以字或词为兴趣区的眼动指标	①单一注视时间 ②首次注视时间 ③第二次注视时间 ④凝视时间 ⑤离开目标后的首次注视时间 ⑥回视时间 ⑦总注视时间
	以短语或句子为兴趣区的眼动指标	⑧第一遍阅读时间 ⑨向前阅读时间 ⑩第二遍阅读时间 ⑪回视路径阅读时间 ⑫重读时间

续表

空间维度的眼动指标	⑬眼跳距离 ⑭注视位置 ⑮注视次数 ⑯跳读率 ⑰再注视比率 ⑱回视次数
其他指标	⑲瞳孔直径 ⑳兴趣区

限于篇幅，在此只对其中的主要指标加以阐述。

一、兴趣区与注视位置

兴趣区是研究者确定的目标区域，可以是字词、短语、句子等。对于学生来说，"兴趣区"定在句子成分、动词、语法成分标志信号词上，会加快阅读速度。[①]

注视位置是指注视点所处的位置，在阅读中，注视和跳动交互进行，当前的注视位置是前一次眼跳的落点位置(landing site)，也是下一次眼跳的起跳位置(launch site)。注视位置主要受词长和起跳位置的影响，在英语阅读中，如果单词较短，有4—5个字符，其注视位置经常位于单词(词语)的中心，如果单词较长，注视位置一般处于词语中心偏左的位置。

二、瞳孔直径

原始的瞳孔直径的眼动数据指在当前刺激情境下读者的瞳孔直径大小，但在分析眼动数据时多采用瞳孔直径的变化值。影响瞳孔直径的因素有：感情、亮度、颜色、疲劳程度、视觉刺激的空间频率等。瞳孔直径

---

① 许斌.核心素养理念下的初中英语阅读教学策略探析[J].新课程,2022(06):43.

的变化被用来推测认知加工的努力程度或认知负荷的大小。一般来说,学生在分析复杂句子时会比分析简单句子时"瞳孔直径变化"更大,在阅读理解过程中,瞳孔大小的变化可以作为心理加工的强度(intensity)指标。句子理解难度越高,记忆负荷量越大,瞳孔也会放得越大。瞳孔直径的变化存在词频效应:低频词加工时,瞳孔直径变化幅度显著大于高频词。瞳孔的大小也会随感情变化,对特别感兴趣的事物,瞳孔会自动放大。学生阅读时选择自己感兴趣的材料,瞳孔就会放大,让更多的光进入。瞳孔就好比一个窗帘,兴趣越大,大脑便会将这个窗帘拉得越开,以便接收更多的光线和信息。

三、眼跳与眼跳距离

眼跳是指眼球从一注视点到另一注视点的运动。单词、短语可以有多个注视点。眼跳距离是指从眼跳开始到此次眼跳结束之间的距离。眼跳距离大,说明学生在眼跳前的注视中所获得的信息相对较多,阅读速度较快。研究发现随着文章难度的加大,学生的眼跳距离变短。在视觉搜索任务中眼跳距离比注视时间更能解释个体成绩的变异和提高。因此,眼跳距离可以看作反映阅读效率和阅读材料难度的指标。

四、首次注视时间

首次注视时间(first fixation duration)指在首次阅读中,对某兴趣区内的首个注视点的注视时间,不用考虑该兴趣区有多少个注视点。注意这里需要区分几个概念:兴趣区可以是单词、汉字,也可以是词组、短语等;注视点不等于某一个具体的单词、汉字。如在图1-1中,注视点①③④⑤⑨—⑫都是首次注视点。在当前的阅读眼动研究中,"首次注视时间"是常用指标,能有效反映词汇通达的早期阶段特征。

影响首次注视时间长短的因素有:正字法特征、语音特性、词汇特征(词频、词长、词的可预测性等)、语境限制等。

泥石流	常常	发生	在	半	干旱	山区	或	高原	冰川区
①→②	③		④→⑤						
⑥→	⑦			⑧→⑨	⑩	⑪	⑫→⑬		

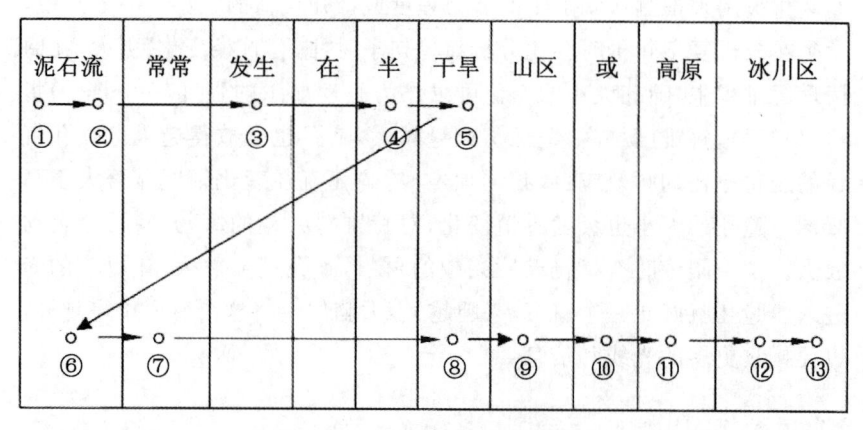

图 1-1　假设的眼动轨迹图

学生对歧义句中歧义单词的首次注视时间比没有歧义的句子中同一位置单词的首次注视时间长。由于学生对低频单词比较陌生，所以如果比较"首次注视时间"这个指标，低频单词的会比高频单词的长。首次注视时间代表了对字的早期识别过程以及对字的加工难度。

五、第二次注视时间

当学生第一遍阅读某个兴趣区时，"第二次注视时间"（second fixation duration）是指在图 1-1 中注视点②和⑬上的注视时间。如果某个兴趣区在第一遍阅读过程中还有第三次、第四次注视，即同一个兴趣区内，还有第三个、第四个注视点出现在第一次阅读过程中，那么这些注视点的持续时间也作为第二次注视时间来统计。一般情况下，影响"第二次注视时间"的因素是："首次注视"的持续时间和落点位置。如果"首次注视点"落在词语的起始字母的位置上，那么"首次注视"时间就会比较短，但是随后的"第二次注视时间"往往较长。如果"首次注视点"落在词语的中心位置上，则"首次注视"时间较长，这种情况下，第二次注视时间会较短。注意点的位置不一定正好与某一个单词整体相吻合，最有可能是落在较长单词或短语的某个部分上，这样就有一种可能的情况，某个较长的单词或短语可能有几个注视点。

六、单一注视时间

单一注视时间是指在第一遍阅读过程,从左到右的句子阅读,兴趣区内有且只有一次注视时的注视时间,如图 1-1 中注视点③④⑤⑨⑩和⑪。

七、凝视时间

第一遍阅读中,某个兴趣区内会包括不止一个注视点,即学生在这个兴趣区内注视了多次,多次注视的时间之和为凝视时间。如图 1-1 兴趣区"泥石流"内有两个注视点①和②,两者的时间之和即为凝视时间(gaze duration),如果眼睛注视点始终没有跳出"泥石流"这个兴趣区,并且在第一遍阅读过程中发生回视的情况,那么回视注视点的注视时间也算为凝视时间。凝视时间反映初始的阅读情况。

八、回视

回视(regression)指在对关键区域的第一遍注视后,对该区域进行再阅读。图 1-1 中的注视点⑥就属于对"泥石流"的回视。回视有利于对文章进行更深层的加工。出现回视的原因有这么几种情况:对所读内容的理解产生困难、出现了语意错误、阅读时漏掉了重要内容,但还记得在什么位置;阅读歧义句时也出现回视;句子中使用了"前后照应"这种语法现象时也容易出现回视。"前后照应"是英语语句的主要衔接手段。学生在阅读过程中有意识地主动应用衔接手段,提高对衔接手段的敏感度,加以适当的回视,会有助于提高阅读效率。①

九、回视时间与回视次数

回视时间(regression time)和回视次数(regression count)是反映词

---

① 孟留军. 大学英语阅读实训[M]. 合肥:安徽大学出版社,2018.

汇后期加工过程的指标。回视分为两种情况：一种是在第一遍阅读过程中，没有出这个兴趣区就发生的回视，这种回视时间归为凝视时间。另外一种是在第一遍阅读过程中眼光的注视点已经跳出了兴趣区，然后发生回视，又回到原来的兴趣区，这种回视时间不归为凝视时间。如图1-1中注视点⑥的注视时间即为兴趣区"泥石流"的回视时间，从⑤到⑥的运动就是回视。回视有两个指标：一个叫回视出（regressions out），一个叫回视入（regressions in）。回视入，也称为"回视进来"，指从后面的区域进入这个区域。"回视进来"是一个比较晚期的指标，发现问题了，需要解决问题。回视出，在某个区域，遇到困难了，需要回视前面的内容，发生回视出，是一个比较早期的指标，发现问题了，需要出去。回视是为对文章进行更深层次的加工。

回视是学生对已经阅读过的信息进行再加工的过程。回视有两种：词内回视和词间回视。词内回视是指在一个词语内由右向左的眼跳，反映词汇的通达过程；词间回视是指从当前注视词向过去已经读过的某个词语的眼跳，反映句子整合的加工过程，即对一句内几个词语间关系的理解过程。

回视次数包括两种类型：回视出次数（regression out count）和回视入次数（regression in count）。回视出次数指注视点当前在兴趣区A，以A区域为起始位置，像以前的B区发生回视的次数，回视出次数反映了学生在A区域发现问题的情况。回视入次数指以B区域为注视点的降落位置，回视落入B区域的次数。

十、总注视时间

总注视时间（total fixation duration）也被称为总停留时间（total dwell time）、总阅读时间（total reading time）和总观看时间（total viewing time），是学生在兴趣区内所有注视点上持续时间的总和。总注视时间不包括学生对兴趣区之前内容的回视时间，因此不等于学生对兴趣区的"完全加工时间"。比如"干旱"的总注视时间是⑤⑧的注视时间之和，不包括⑥⑦的注视时间。

十一、注视次数

注视次数(number of fixations)是指兴趣区被注视的总次数。该指标能有效反映阅读材料的认知加工负荷,认知负荷较大的阅读材料,注视次数也更多。注视次数指标又可以细分为向前注视次数(number of forward fixations)和回视注视次数(number of regressive fixations)。前者只计算由向前眼跳引发的注视次数,后者则只计算由回视引发的注视次数。

十二、跳读率

跳读率(skipping rate)指在第一遍阅读中,某个兴趣区被跳读的概率。概率是对随机事件发生的可能性的度量,用来描述 N 个读者在阅读同一内容时,对某一个兴趣区所发生的阅读现象。跳读率是针对第一遍阅读中的某特定兴趣区而言的,可用公式表示为:

跳读率＝被跳读的频率:(被跳读频率＋被注视频率)

影响跳读的最主要因素是词长。与较长的词相比,短词更有可能被跳读。1 个字母构成的单词被跳读率约为 80％,3 个字母构成的词语为 60％,5 个字母构成的词语为 30％,7 个字母或更长的词语为 10％。其次,词的预期性也影响跳读率。预期性高的词会更容易被跳读。当一个词语被跳读时,跳读前的注视时间往往较长。

第四节 阅读能力的本质

开始阅读时,我们往往会很快做出一些初步判断,其中多为无意识行为。例如,拿起报纸阅读头版时,我们往往会综合使用搜寻、概要阅读和快速浏览这些策略。我们的阅读是为了搜寻信息,但也是为了快速读完报纸,因为极少有人逐行逐句地读报纸。

一开始，我们或许会在头版搜寻某个我们期待的报道。当通过浏览标题找到目标内容时，我们可能会快速查看文章的长度，然后可能通读几段（适当受报道文体的影响，即这是一个关于何事、何人、何时、何地、为何和如何的报道）。读到某处时，我们会决定是否已获得足够信息，然后或许会停止阅读，或许会快速浏览其余内容，以确保不错过信息量大的内容。

在其他场合，通常是学术或专业阅读，我们有时会将来自多渠道、多种资源、复杂、长文本各部分或一篇普通文本及其附表的信息综合起来。这种阅读迥异于搜索式阅读、快速阅读或一般性理解的阅读。在这些情况下，为达到更有效的综合理解，需要树立更有批判性的系列目标：阅读者需要记住相近或相反的信息点，评估信息的重要性，并建立信息的组织框架。

我们可能阅读一本小说、一个短篇故事、一篇报纸文章或某类报道，目的是获取文本信息、消遣以及利用信息达到某一目的等。阅读的整体目标并非记住大部分具体细节，而是很好地掌握其主旨大意及支撑性内容，并将其大意与背景知识恰当地联系起来。所有这些及其他阅读方式，都要在全面解释阅读过程的基础上才能得到解释。

一、寻找简单信息及快速浏览

寻找简单信息是一种常见的阅读能力，尽管有研究者认为这是一种相对独立的认知过程。鉴于阅读中经常用到该能力，因此视之为阅读能力。在阅读中搜寻信息，我们通常会通过扫读全文来寻找某个单词、信息或几个代表性词组。例如，我们经常在电话通讯录上查找关键信息，如地址或电话号码。读文章时，我们有时会放慢阅读速度来理解某个句子或词组，以便找到线索来判断我们读的是不是我们需要的那一页、节或章。[1] 同样，略读（快速阅读文本以获得大致理解）也是众多阅读任务中的一种，而它本身也是一种有助于阅读的技能。从根本上说，略读需要多种技能配合来猜测重要信息的位置，然后使用基本阅读理解技能获得文章大意。

---

[1] 格拉伯,斯托勒. 英语阅读教学与研究[M]. 赵燕,译. 天津:天津大学出版社,2020.

二、在文本阅读中获取信息

以信息获取为目的的阅读通常发生在学术或专业领域中,人们需要从某一文本中获取大量信息。这种阅读需要下列三种能力。
(1)记住主旨大意及用来阐述大意的支撑性细节。
(2)识别并构建文本信息组织的修辞框架。
(3)将文本与读者的知识库联系起来。

以信息获取为目的的阅读通常比以一般性理解为目的的阅读慢些(主要是因为需要反复阅读和反思来记忆信息)。此外,比起后者,它需要做出更有力的推断,从而将文本信息与背景知识联系起来,如将某人物、事件或概念与其他已知的人物、事件或概念联系起来,或将可能的原因与已知的事件联系起来。

三、整合信息、写作和评判文本

以信息整合为目的的阅读还要判断那些相互支持或彼此冲突的信息的相对重要性,以及为囊括多渠道信息而重构修辞框架的可能性。这些技能无一例外都需要对所读信息进行评价,以便读者能够决定要整合哪些信息,以及如何整合这些信息来实现自己的目标。在这一点上,为了写作的阅读和为了文本评价的阅读都可能是为了整合信息的某种阅读形式,都需要从文本中选择、评价并表达信息。

四、以一般性理解为目的的阅读

对于熟练流利的阅读者来说,一般性阅读理解意味着快速、自动地处理语言,有效把握大意,并在有限的时间内有效组合多种信息处理过程。对于流利阅读者来说,这些能力都是自动发生的,因此都是很自然的,即流利阅读者运用这些能力是不加思考的。然而,二语语境中的学生在一定时间内难以流利地阅读较长文本,这正说明了一般性理解阅读的复杂性。因为要高效处理信息,所以一般性理解阅读有时比以学习为目的的阅读更难掌握,而后者往往被认为是难度更大的一般性理解阅读。

在界定流利阅读之前，我们想讨论一下阅读中最常用的两个术语：技能和策略。对我们来说，技能代表语言处理能力。相对来说，这些能力不需要读者有意识地调动知识和能力，都是自动组合使用的（如识别单词和句子分析）。

教育心理学对技能的讨论大都视之为目标驱动型任务的学习成果，是逐步并最终成为自动行为的。策略通常被认为是读者能用意识控制的一系列能力，虽然这一定义可能并不完全正确。实际上，对于流利阅读者来说，许多被普遍认为是策略的能力都是相对自动完成的（如在阅读中跳过不认识的单词、重复阅读以便再次确立文本意义）。因此，技能与策略之间的差异并非十分明显，这正是由阅读的本质（而非其定义）决定的。完整定义一下，阅读过程指的是一种认知活动，涉及技能、策略、注意力资源、知识资源及上述的综合运用。能力是一个统称，它涵盖了理解能力、策略和读者能接触到的知识资源。例如，在很多情况下，技能本可以作为策略来学习，但实际上却是完全自动完成的（如在头脑中概括一个新闻报道并讲给朋友听）。然而，对于阅读能力来说，"策略"依然是一个重要概念。为了方便定义，策略指的是一种潜在的、能够被有意识地反思的能力，它反映了读者在阅读中解决问题或实现某个具体目标的意愿。

第二章　英语阅读与英语语言知识

英语阅读的顺利开展不仅需要学生掌握一定的阅读方法与阅读技巧,而且还需要学生具备一定的英语语言基础知识,如此才能顺利开展阅读活动。在阅读过程中,学生首先需要处理的是词汇知识,进而结合句法知识、语篇知识来掌握所读篇章的主题。为此,本章就针对这方面内容展开深入分析。

第一节　英语阅读与词汇知识

众所周知,英语学习中遇到的最普遍问题是词汇量问题,词汇是英语听、说、读、写、译多种语言技能的基础。虽然我国的学生从小学甚至是幼儿园就开始学习英语,背诵英语单词,但是经历了小学、中学直至大学时,仍然要不断地扩大词汇量,有的学生到大学毕业时能掌握四五千基本英语词汇,有的人掌握得还要多,但是一到实际生活、工作和学习中,大部分人还是觉得所掌握的英语词汇量远远不能满足自己的需要,即便英语学习到了硕士生、博士生的水平,依然在为英语词汇量发愁。词汇量的大小直接关系到一个人英语阅读能力的好坏、阅读速度的快慢和阅读理解的准确与否。

其实,英语词汇的掌握大体可以分为两类,即对认知性词汇的掌握和对复用性词汇的掌握。认知性词汇主要用于提高接受性技能(receptive skills),即一个人的认知性词汇量越大,其阅读、听和英译汉等信息输入大脑的接受能力就提高得越快,而其接受能力则使其在信息输入时会比其他人更能准确迅速地读懂文字材料,领会口头信息,把握对方即信息输出者的意图,对所接受的材料达到深层全面的理解;复用性词汇主要用于改进产出性技能(productive skills),即一个人的复用性词汇越丰富,他的说、写、汉译英等信息输出的表达能力就越强,从而可以使自己的口语表达和书面表达不仅用词多样化而且准确达意,使交流能正常有序而又有效地进行下去。

但是,许多人往往并不清楚这一点,他们笼统地认为一个人词汇量的大小就是指一个人头脑中所能记住的词汇的多少,因而一旦提到要增加词汇量的问题,他们自然而然想到的就是要多记多背英语单词。这种观点虽然看似有道理,对幼儿、儿童或少年等机械记忆力比较好的人来说,这种看法是合乎情理的,但是对于许多成年人来说,我们的机械记忆能力越来越差,完全靠死记硬背来扩充词汇量是不现实的。而且,随着年龄的增长、阅历的增加、知识的扩充,我们经常会发现在进行英语阅读时有些单词明明自己知道是什么意思,可是按照这种意思来理解文章却发现上下文内容根本风马牛不相及。这是因为英语一词多义的现象非常普遍。① 例如,英语单词 later 大家看到以后没有谁会说是生词,都知道它表示"迟到的、晚的",但是,它还可以在不同的场合用来表示最近的、最新的(如 the latest news),上一任的、前任的(如 the late American president Clinton),已故的、去世的(如 late Richard Nixon)。

总体来说,作为一般读者,想要读懂一般常识性和生活中常用的文字材料,我们应该掌握的英语词汇量是 4000—5000 个左右,这个数目既包括认知性词汇又包括复用性词汇。另外,仅仅孤立地背会记住这些词汇还不够,还要领会式掌握 500 个左右的常用词组,了解熟悉一定数量的常用词根和词缀,并能根据构词法知识和上下文语境识别分析和推断出常见派生词的词义。

在英语教学、学习和辅导的过程中,我们常常会发现许多学生和英语学习者以及英语读者在英语词汇学习方面有以下一些问题。

第一个问题是许多人有一定的认知性词汇量,但复用性词汇量还远远不够。这一问题表现在许多学生在进行英语阅读理解、听力训练、英译汉及语法练习时往往能基本读懂、听懂、译出或做对,但在进行英语的口语表达、书面表达包括英语写作或做汉译英时,则词汇匮乏。究其原因,一是头脑中根本没有掌握所需词汇,二是掌握的是认知性的词汇,不

---

① 韩满玲,邓保中. 英语阅读的奥秘[M]. 北京:中国国际广播出版社,2006.

第二章　英语阅读与英语语言知识

是复用性的词汇,因此许多学生经常抱怨"我知道那些词,但我就是想不起来要用它",或是"这些词别人写出来说出来我都知道,可我就是不会用"。其实,只要做一个英语阅读中的有心人,我们就可以在词汇积累方面得到很大收获。例如下面这个小段落,你不妨阅读一下,想一想能从这四句话中学到什么,将来既可以对自己的阅读有帮助,又可以提高自己的英语写作表达和口头表达的能力。

Imaginations were fired. Men dreamed of going to work in their own personal helicopters. People anticipated that vertical flight transports would carry millions of passengers as do the airliners of today. Such fantastic expectations were not fulfilled.

大家是否发现了就在这四句话中,作者用了四个表示"想象、梦想、期望"等的同义词:imaginations,dreamed of,anticipated,expectations。能够发现这一点还只是迈出了第一步,我们可否由此再进一步地引申一下,将来自己不管是在书面上还是口头上要用英语"想象、梦想、期望"的时候,能否想到除了可以使用这几个词本身外,还可以改头换面地利用它们的衍生词,如 imagine,imaginative,imaginary,imaginable,anticipatable,anticipation,expect,expectable 等词,以使自己的英语写作用词多样化,显示出自己的英语词汇量呢?

在英语教学中,当要求学生写一篇关于计算机在英语教学中有何用处的作文时,许多学生通篇文章中反复使用 use,一些学生用到了 utilization,helpful,useful,do good 等词汇和短语,只有极少数学生用了 apply,application,employ,employment 等也可表达这一意思的同义词、近义词,从而使自己所写的文章用词丰富多样化。姑且不提他们所用的这些同义词、近义词是否得当,仅是他们这种敢于和能够利用自己的认知性词汇从而将其变为复用性词汇的精神也是可嘉的。另外,许多人在写作和口语表达及做汉译英时,所用的词汇量还仅仅局限于两三千的基本英语词汇量,虽然能进行基本的信息交流,但只相当于以英语为母语的中学生的英语水平,因此许多人的复用性词汇量还有待于大幅度地提高。复用性词汇量的扩大直接影响到一个人英语阅读能力的高低和英语表达能力的优劣。

第二个问题是有些人掌握的英语词汇量虽然不少,但仍处在一词一义阶段,忽视了英语词汇中一词多义、多词同义或多词近义的现象,也忽略了对近形词的辨析和准确掌握。

许多英语学习者在进行英语阅读训练或做英译汉练习时,常会有"这篇文章中没有一个生词,但我就是看不懂"或是"这篇文章一点也不难,没有生词,可是翻译成汉语后怎么一点都不通呢?"这些感觉。带有这些疑问的读者其实大部分都是因为他们在单词的掌握过程中,只关注了所学所记单词的第一个含义,而不清楚或不去掌握这些单词的第二种、第三种……,以及引申含义等。

因此,在不同的英语阅读材料中、在有很大差异的上下文语境中,他们都用该单词的第一个语义去理解,在语境不符合第一语义的情况下,自然就会产生误解了。这种现象有些英语词汇学习者注意到了,并且在学习中有意地从多角度来掌握词汇,而另一些人则根本没放在心上或是对此现象毫无觉察,仍采取僵化的、机械死记硬背的方法,因此在学习上和应试中产生了很多困难。如下面这段文章:

Scattered around the globe are more than 100 small regions of isolated volcanic activity known to geologists as hot spots. Unlike most of the world's volcanoes, they are not always found at the boundaries of the great drifting plates that make up the earth's surface; on the contrary, many of them lie deep in the interior of a plate. Most of the hot spots move only slowly, and in some cases the movement of the plates past them has left trails of dead volcanoes. The hot spots and their volcanic trails are milestones that mark the passage of the plates.

其中的单词 plate 和 passage,很多学生在初次阅读时,在头脑中反映出来的两个词的语义分别是"盘子、大碟子"和"段落",但通过阅读这两个词所在的语境上下文,其实不难猜出两个单词的语义应分别是指"大陆板块"和"经过、漂流过"等意,因为如果用这两个词的第一语义则这两个单词所表达的含义与文章上下文毫无连贯一致性,而且风马牛不相及。这就是一词多义在英语阅读中给人们带来的困难。另外,对多词同义或多词近义以及近形词疏于辨析和确切掌握,会对一个人的接收信息能力和产出信息能力都带来影响,即忽视了这种词的掌握,在听、说、读、写、译各方面都会产生错误理解和不正确表达的现象。

第三个问题是掌握了词汇的含义,但不重视词汇的词性及固定搭配,即忽视了词汇、词组的用法。因此,在英语阅读时对词汇和短语的理解以及使用等方面容易产生错误,降低了自己的认知性词汇量和复用性词汇量,也影响了自己的真实词汇量。

第二章　英语阅读与英语语言知识

学习第二语言的词汇不是简单地记忆目的语词汇在母语中的对应译词或单词的定义，而是要学习单个词与目的语中其他词在整个文化背景下的各种各样的意义联系。因此，英语单词的学习不能孤立起来，只为记单词而单纯地学习词汇是不对的，这只是对词汇进行的低层次加工，记忆效果不佳。

对于在没有英语语言学习环境，即不是身处在讲英语的国家的中国英语学习者来说，最佳的掌握词汇的途径就是大量阅读英文原版小说、英语原版报刊和英语原版教科书等。这样不仅可以广泛掌握大量词汇，了解词的意义和用法，还可以开阔自己的思路，置身于特定的文化背景和语境中来有效地记忆认知性词汇和复用性词汇，最终达到有效地掌握和扩大英语词汇总量的目的。下面详细地为大家介绍一下英语阅读与英语构词法、记词法和猜词法的关系与运用。

一、英语阅读与构词法

了解英语词汇的构词规律对扩大英语词汇量、记忆英语陌生词汇以及猜测新词、难词和生词非常有帮助。尤其在我们进行英语文章阅读时，往往会遇到许多生词与难词，如果懂得一些英语构词法知识，则可以根据构词法知识比较轻松、较为准确地推断出难词与生词的基本义，从而为理解文章整体内容和要点信息拓开道路。

英语中常见的构词法主要有以下几种。

（一）合成式构词法

了解合成式构词法不仅可以帮助大家记忆新词汇，猜测新词汇的意思，还可以帮助大家在表达某个汉语意思却不知道用哪个英语单词来表述时创造出一个新词来。① 例如：

中国人民大学出版社出版的《研究生英语精读教程》上册第 8 课中有一个生词 jellyware，我们查遍各种词典都找不到这个单词，但是根据文章的标题"Computer Illiteracy"以及文章内容中多次提到计算机中的

---

① 韩建全，陈晓霞. 大学英语阅读[M]. 成都：西南交通大学出版社，2015.

常用语 hardware(硬件), software(软件), 结合 jellyware 这个生词所在的上下文, 你可否猜出这个单词的大致含义呢? 相关上下文如下:

It was pointed out by a computer wag that a computerized system consists of three subsystems: hardware, software, and jellyware.

Hardware is the computer itself—the collection of slightly impure chunks of silicon dioxide and other metal oxides that sometimes conduct electricity and sometimes don't, but never conduct it very well. Basically, hardware is mostly sand with some metal and some organic plastic material to hold it together.

Software consists of the instructions necessary in order for the hardware to do things. The instructions are nothing more than signals indicating that certain pieces of hardware are to turn themselves on or off in specific sequences at specific times in specific areas of the hardware. The basic instructions are written or given in binary terms—on or off—and other software elements translate this to and from the more complex language used by the next element in the system.

Jellyware is the human being who tells the hardware what to do, who gives the hardware its data, who utilizes the output of the hardware, who writes the software, and who uses the output of the software. Jellyware itself is a computer consisting of hardware and software. Jellyware is mostly water with specific and small amounts of impurities in certain locations. The jellyware's software is mostly preprogrammed (ROM in hardware/software terms) with some RAM that is inputted as a result of experience.

Hardware and jellyware differ only in the fact that hardware is made up of crystalline structures while jellyware consists of colloidal structures. The jellyware's operating systems appear to function in the parallel mode while those of the hardware operate in a series mode. However, the output of jellyware is one-channel sequential and series in form. Like hardware, jellyware can do only one thing at a time.

读完这段短文之后, 大家是否猜出来了 jellyware 的具体含义是指"人类的大脑"或是"人类自己"呢? 而这个单词源于 jelly, 其意思是"果冻、肉冻", 而人的大脑的外观质地与"果冻、肉冻"有相似之处, 于是文章的作者就根据合成式构词法自己创造了这个生词,我们不妨将此词译为"脑件"。

合成词在我们的日常生活和工作学习中随处可见,而且大部分利用合成式构成的新词汇的含义我们大体上都能够猜出来。

(二)词根词缀式构词法/衍生式构词法

词根词缀式构词法(affixation/derivation)是英语构词法中最为重要的一种方式。例如:

词根-vis-/-vid-,此词根的意思是"look,view(看)",但-vis-和-vid-本身都不可单独使用。在句子或文章段落中,必须与前缀如 re-、super-等,与后缀如-ual、-ible、-ion 等,或与前后缀 tele-和-ion 等构成以下具有独立性的英语单词。

revise(审校、修订、温习、再看)

supervise(监督、督导、高高在上地看着)

visual(与看有关的,视力的、视觉的)

visible(可见的,能被看到的)

invisibility(不可见性,不可见度)

vision(视力、眼光、洞察力、看到的奇景、奇观)

television(看到的远处的东西、电视)

visage(看到的东西,外观,脸,面容,外表)

vis(a)(看,审查,审查后签字,签证,签准)

evident(e-的意思与前缀 ex-一致,表示出来 out 的意思,-ent 是形容词后缀,此词的本义是看得出来的,引申义为:明显的,明白的)

provide(pro-这个前缀的意思是:预先、前,-vid-的意思是看见,因此,此词的本义是"预先见到而做准备",引申义为:做准备,预防,提供,装备,供给)

improvident(im-这个前缀的意思是:无、没有,-ent 是形容词后缀,因此,此词的含义是:无远见的)

video(vid-的意思是:看、观看、可观看的图像,因此,此词的意思是:电视、电视的,可视的)

videophone(电视电话,可视电话)

videocast(电视广播

自由式词根也是由几个字母组成的具有固定语义的语言单位。与粘着式词根不同的是,自由式词根本身也是一个单词,可以独立使用于句子和段落中,也可以与前缀或后缀或前后缀结合以后构成一个意义不同的新词。例如:

词根 claim,此词根既是词根,又是单词,意思与"喊叫"有关,与之相关的单词如:

claim 声称、要求、自称

exclaim（ex-这个前缀的意思是 out,出来、外出,因此此词的意思是:呼喊、惊叫、大叫）

acclaim（ac-这个前缀的意思是表示加强意义的,claim 的意思是叫、呼喊,因此,acclaim 的意思是:欢呼、喝彩）

proclaim 宣布、宣告、声明

declaim 做慷慨激昂的演说、朗诵

disclaim 否认、拒绝承认

在以这种词根词缀构词法生成的单词词根中,粘着式词根相对来说比重要大得多。英语单词数量庞大,可多达几十万。但常用的词根只有约 300 多个,掌握一个词根,就可以认识和推测出几个、十几个甚至几十个、上百个单词。因此,词根的掌握在英语词汇学习中占有重要的地位。

英语单词的词缀也分为两类:前缀和后缀。前缀通常是改变词汇含义的,一个单词或词根加上前缀后就可以生成语义不同的单词。后缀则是改变词汇的词性的,一个单词或词根加上后缀后就可以生成语法功能和词性不同但语义相近或相同的新单词。常见的前缀和后缀各约有 100 多个。掌握了这些常用词缀后对快速提高英语词汇量非常有帮助。例如:

前缀:fore 表示"前、先、预先",那么我们便不难猜出以下几个单词的含义了。

foretell 预言

forehead 前额

forearm 前臂、小臂

foretime 已往、过去

forefather 前人、祖先

foreleg 前腿

foresee 预见、先见

foreword 前言、序言
foreknow 先知、预知
foreground 前景
forerun 先驱、前驱
forepayment 预先付款

后缀如-able,-ible,-uble 表示"可……的""能……的"或具有某种性质的,以下这些单词的记忆和词义推测可以轻松实现。

knowable 可知的
readable 可读的
useable 可用的
movable 可移动的
sensible 可感觉的
changeable 可变的
lovable 可爱的
dependable 可靠的
adaptable 可适应的
visible 可视的

(三)转化式构词法

转化式构词法(conversion)是指一般情况下原词汇的词形即词汇的拼写形式保持不变,词义维持原义或稍有引申发展,而词性进行转变。名词、形容词和副词等都有转化的现象,其中以名词转化为动词最常见。例如:

I breakfast at seven every morning.(这里 breakfast 即由原来的名词"早餐"转化为了动词"吃早餐"。)

The boy is going to summer at seaside next week.(这里 summer 也由原来的名词"夏天"转化为了动词"度过夏天"。)

Please empty the box.(这里 empty 由形容词"空的"转化为了动词"倒空"。)

随着英语的日益发展,转化式构词法越来越常见,它是简洁、生动地表达信息的一种重要手段。了解这种构词法,对根据上下文准确理解词义尤为重要。

(四)混合式构词法/拼缀式构词法

混合式构词法(blending)是指从两个独立的单词中各取掉一部分字母,将剩下的部分混合在一起构成一个新的词汇。这种构词法与合成式构词法有些相近,如利用这两种构词法创造出的新词通常可以从单词的构成词汇的含义中推断出新生词汇的含义。但二者也有不同之处,如合成式构词法所包含的基本词汇的词形不变化,而且合成式单词的构成词汇可以是多个单词的组合,hard-to-get-to place(难以到达的地方)。混合式构词法的组成成分只有两个,如下列混合式构词法创造出的词汇。

smog＝smoke＋fog（烟雾）
motel＝motor＋hotel（汽车旅馆）
brunch＝breakfast＋lunch（早午餐）
Amex＝American＋exchange（美证券交易所）
comsat＝communications＋satellite（通信卫星）
Chinglish＝Chinese＋English（汉语式英语）

(五)截短式构词法

截短式构词法(clipping)是指将多音节词或拼写中字母较多的单词截掉一部分,从而形成词义不变,拼写与原词既有相关性又有所不同的新词。截短式构词法有三种截取方式。

截前留后式,如:

plane＝airplane/aeroplane（飞机）
phone＝telephone（电话）
bus＝trolleybus（公共汽车）

截后留前式,如:

ad＝advertisement（广告）
lab＝laboratory（实验室）
exam＝examination（考试）

前后截留中间稍做变动式,如:

flu＝influenza（流行性感冒）

fridge=refrigerator（电冰箱）

fax=facsimile（传真机或传真）

　　截短式构词法生成的词汇虽然在英语总词汇量中占的比重不是很大，但在平时的生活、工作和学习中也时常会见到这种词汇，所以大家应该学会能够根据这种构词法知识并结合上下文内容，猜测推断出生词的基本大意。

(六)缩略式构词法

　　缩略式构词法(abbreviating)是现代英语中的一种主要构词手段，是指从原词中摘取少则一个字母、多则几个字母来替代原词的构词方式，这种字母的摘取大部分会保留单词的第一个字母，而其他部分则无定式，或采用首尾字母，或采用合成式单词的几个构成词汇的首字母，或采用词根词缀式构词法形成的新单词中词根或词缀的首字母来组合替代原来的词汇。由于应用这种构词法造词简练，使用方便，我们可以经常在科技文章和报刊的文章中见到以这种构词法生成的单词，在日常生活和工作中这种词汇也屡见不鲜。例如：

m=meter（米）

120 m/h=120 mile/hour（120 英里/小时）

kg=kilogram（千克）

Ltd=limited（有限的）

P.S.=postscript（后记、附笔）

St.=Saint（圣）或 Street（街道）

Rd=Road（路）

Xmas=Christmas（圣诞节）

(七)杜撰式构词法

　　杜撰式构词法(nonce word)又称为生造词、臆造词、临时语或仿词。是作者在一定的语言上下文中为表达一种特殊的用法或特别的意义而创造的偏离常规的变异词语，是一种语言文字上的创造，可以使读者通过正常的指代而思索新词的言外之意。例如：

根据 Literature 杜撰出 Litterature "垃圾文学"；

根据 No Olympics 杜撰出 Nolympics "反申办奥运";

根据 Day & Night 杜撰出 Day & Nite (ditto) "日夜营业";

根据 Car Care 杜撰出的 Kar Kare "汽车保养"等。

了解了以上几种英语单词构词法,可以为我们大家学习和了解新词汇奠定基础,也为我们记忆词汇和猜测生词的基本含义提供了一些方法和依据。

二、英语阅读与猜词法

在我们进行英语阅读时,总是会遇到一些情况使我们没有办法去查词典和其他工具书,或是即便可以利用词典和工具书的情况下,我们却无法在所用的参考工具书中找到想要查找的生词,在这些情况下,猜测和推断词汇的技巧就显得尤为重要了,而且我们认为,英语学习到了一定的阶段,词汇的积累不应该再靠死记硬背,而是应该通过大量阅读来在文章中掌握一定量的新词和生词,而且英语学习到了一定的层次时,衡量一个人英语水平的高低,应该说很大程度上要看这个人对生词的推断猜测能力。

在阅读各种英语文章时,大家往往会遇到一些从来没有见过或是从没学过的生词,遇到这种情况该怎么办呢?大多数人会搬出词典之类的辅助工具查找生词的词义。在平时情况下,也许我们可以参看这些工具书或工具,但在英语测试中该怎么办呢?大多数英语测试时是不许翻看参考材料和工具书的。在这种情况下,我们只能靠猜测和推断词汇的含义了。英语词汇的猜测必须有一定词汇量做基础,如需掌握 3000 个左右的基本常用单词,再辅以前面所讲的构词法,参照文章上下文的内容,其实有很多生词还是能够推断出其基本含义的。虽然有时可能推断的不是其百分之百的确切含义,但猜测出生词的百分之五十或是百分之六十的基本意思还是可能实现的。这样对我们了解文章内容也有一定的帮助。在阅读理解中,词汇的猜测方法也多种多样,下面介绍几种常见的猜词方法。

(一)根据构词法猜词

英语构词法可以帮助大家很快猜出生词的基本含义,有时在没有上

第二章　英语阅读与英语语言知识

下文提示的情况下，利用构词法猜词就显得更为重要了。利用这种猜词法首先要熟悉英语中的各种构词法和其规律，其次要掌握一定量的词根和词缀，这样才可能在猜测生词词义时把握得较为准确。例如：

They had eleven crude houses for protection against the severe winter. Seven were for families, and four were for communal use.

No one knows for sure what the world would be like in the year 2001. Many books have been written about the future. But the 19th century French novelist Jules Verne may be called a futurologist in the fullest sense of the word.

在第一个句子中，大家知道词根 com- 的意思是"共同的、一起的"，而 commune 是指"公社，社区"。因此，利用词根词缀式构词法，便可很快猜出 communal 的意思是"公社的，公共的，社区的"。

在第二个句子中，我们仍然可以利用词根词缀式构词法来猜词。其中，future 我们知道意思是"未来"，而 -ology 是表示"学科，科学"的后缀，-ist 则表示"……主义者，……学家，做某事的人"，所以 futurologist 的意思是"未来学家"。

(二)根据句子中的语法知识猜词

英语语法知识对猜测词汇含义也有很大帮助，知道在一个英语句子中，同位语或同位语从句，定语或定语从句这些起解释说明、补充限定作用的语法成分往往能为我们猜测某些生词的词义提供线索和提示。例如：

The purpose of the campaign was to catch "ringers", students who take tests for other students.

The explorers decided that this was a fossil of an extinct animal that once lived but does not exist now.

在第一个句子中，ringers 后面有一个同位语，而这个同位语所表达的内容就是 ringers 的意思。句子上下文中指出，ringers 是那些替别的学生考试的学生。因此，ringers 是指"冒名替考者"。

第二句中有两个生词，fossil，extinct。根据 extinct 这个生词后面的定语从句，这种动物以前曾活过，但是现在不存在了。由此可知，extinct 是指"灭绝的，绝种的"。而这种灭绝的动物只能留有"化石"存在了。因此,fossil 的意思是"化石"。

第二节 英语阅读与句法知识

英语阅读理解能力是一种综合能力,在有了一定词汇量的基础后,仍有许多人在阅读时觉得文章具体在介绍什么自己并不十分清楚,即使文章所有的单词都认识。之所以出现这种情况,是因为有些人的语法功底比较薄弱,尤其是对一些特殊句式、复杂句式和长句式的分析和掌握不够准确,感觉句子中的每个单词都认识,但句子表达的含义是什么自己并不知道。因此,若想读懂一个段落、一篇文章,首先要能读懂段落和文章的第二组成部分——句子。

一、英语句子分类

英语的句子按句子结构来分共有三种:简单句、并列句和复合句。其中简单句是三种句子类型中的基础,其他两种句子类型都是由两个或多个简单句构成的。我们在阅读时要训练自己将并列句和复合句分解成简单句的能力,也要培养自己的合并简单句成为一个长句、复杂句并准确理解的能力。在阅读时要注意简单句、并列句和复合句的特征。一般来说,简单句是指由主语、谓语等几个主要句子成分构成而且句中不包括从句的句子。并列句是指由并列连词把两个或两个以上的简单句连在一起的句子,并列连词包括 and, or, but, both … and, as well as, either … or, neither … nor, only 等。复合句是指由一个主句和一个或多个从句构成的句子。例如:

After studying hard, James passed the final examination.(简单句)
Mary became pale from fear of the horrible sight.(简单句)
The party was finally held after being twice postponed.(简单句)
Being tired with walking, the old lady sat down to take a little rest.(简单句)

第二章　英语阅读与英语语言知识

Making up his mind, Jack won't listen to any more argument. (简单句)

Tom was poor in health, and therefore he was unable to run marathon. (并列句)

John must confess his fault, or he will be punished seriously. (并列句)

Fred was well-fitted for that post by character and attainments; only he was rather too young and inexperienced. (并列句)

The sun shone out, and the bats all flew away into their hiding places. (并列句)

Mike did his best to be punctual, but still he was occasionally behind time. (并列句)

What is one man's meat is another man's poison. (复合句)

The question is whether it is proper to do such a thing. (复合句)

The house that we are now living in suits us fine. (复合句)

So far as I know, nothing like that has ever happened before. (复合句)

Whether the plan suggested will succeed or fail depends on how it will be received by those who are most interested in its progress. (复合句)

下面，我们仔细分析一个复合句，以帮助大家加强对比较复杂的句子的理解。例如：

Plainly enough, anyone must realize it who reflects upon the manner in which they reach public office.

在这个句子中，除了词组 reflect upon 表示"思考，考虑"，有些人可能不认识以外，其他的单词绝大部分人都认识，但是能准确理解并翻译出这个句子的意思的人并不多，原因主要是对此句的复杂的句式结构分析不清楚。其实，在这个句子中，主句部分应是简单句 anyone must realize it，每个人都一定会认识到这一点，而 who reflects upon the manner 和 in which they reach public office 是两个定语从句，只不过前一个定语从句修饰代词 anyone，后一个定语从句修饰名词 manner。因为这种分句的存在，尤其是由于前一个定语从句所限定的 anyone 与修饰它的定语从句被分隔了开来，所以全句的语法结构表现得较为复杂，许多人不清楚到底应该怎样分析和理解这个句子。本句的译文应是：

非常明显，那些任何考虑到他们是怎样步入仕途的人一定会认识到这一点的。

二、英语阅读中的特殊句式

在英语文章的阅读过程中,即使了解句子中的每个单词的确切含义,也能清楚地分析出句子中的语法成分和准确地将句子分类,但有时也会出现无法理解或错误理解句子含义的情况,原因是英语文章中经常会出现一些特殊句式。了解这些特殊句式的构成形式对理解句子含义也起着至关重要的作用。下面介绍几种在英语阅读理解测试中常见的特殊句式结构,以帮助大家熟悉并掌握对这些特殊句子的理解。

(一)省略句式

省略句式在英语文章的阅读过程当中往往容易引起误解。省略句通常是为了避免重复,加强表达内容的连贯一致性和逻辑性,把句子前面介绍过的人、事或动作在不影响语义内容的情况下,在句子后面部分中删掉,使之不出现。被省略的部分大多是主语、谓语或构成谓语中的助动词等,还可以是名词、代词或实义动词等词语。许多人在阅读时比较容易将句子中某些词语和成分误解为句子的其他成分。因此,了解省略句的常见形式对提高阅读理解句子的准确性非常有帮助。

1. 谓语部分动词的省略和代替

为避免重复,使句子表达得连贯生动,如果一个动词在句子的前面部分出现过,则后面相同的动词常被省略掉。例如:

Time is only a relative thing:an instant may be an age,an age(may be) an instant.

Then winter came and with it (came) the snow and cold.

第二种动词的省略是复合动词中的助动词或主要部分可被省略。例如:

Winter had come and (had) gone.

The Italian can speak and (can) write Chinese like a Chinese.

Mary knows Mr. Smith,doesn't she (know him)?

第二章　英语阅读与英语语言知识

另外,有些情况下我们可以用动词 do,does 或 did 来代替前面出现过的主要动词。例如:

Many foreigners like Beijing very much, as everybody does (= likes it) who has been there.

And yet the princess wanted to know. You generally do (= want to know) when you are young.

在一些句子中,有时省略掉的词语还包括与动词一起构成谓语、表语等其他词语。例如:

Some people are happy only when doing something, others (are happy) only when idling.

These definitions are necessary because it is important to emphasize that competition between individuals or groups is inevitable in a world of limited resources, but conflict is not (inevitable).

2. 主语的省略

在比较随便的谈话和口语中,当主语是代词时,有时可省略。例如:

(I) Thank you.

(It) sounds like common sense to me.

在口语中某些句子的句首部分,有时不仅可以省略主语,还可以省去更多的词语,只要句子语义清楚,别人能够明白即可。例如:

(Have you) seen the TV programme?

(I am) sorry. (It was) my mistake.

另外,在 there be 句型中,there 虽然不是主语,但在这种句式中的 there 常被省略。例如:

(There) ought to be a law against it.

(Is there) any latest news? —(There's) not much that matters.

除了以上介绍的在口语中主语和其相关部分常被省略以外,在并列句中前后两个句子的主语如果一致的话,后面的一个也可以省略掉。在并列复合句中第二个分句的主语若与前一分句的主语相同也可以省略掉。另外在复合句中,有些从句的主语若与主句的主语一致的话,也可以省略掉。例如:

He makes good resolutions, only (he) never keeps them.

The headmaster came in, but (he) didn't stay long.

For years I have puzzled over the inappropriate communication of simple directions, especially those given me when (I was) touring.

If you think as much of others as (you think) of yourself, you will not make any of these mistakes.

We must avoid this fallacy, (we must) realize that many of our communications are clear only if (they are) already known.

(二)倒装句式

英语文章中句子的正常词序应是"主语＋谓语动词"，但是也有许多情况下要把主语放在谓语动词后，我们称之为倒装。一般情况下常将复合动词中的助动词移到主语之前，主要部分留在后面或省略掉，我们称之为部分倒装，常用于疑问句中。例如：

Have you ever seen the play?

但如果句子中的谓语动词本身是 be 或 have 的简单形式时，则出现此谓语动词与主语的位置完全交换的情况，我们称之为完全倒装。例如：

Have you anything like this one?

Are you a teacher of English?

在表示虚拟语气的句子中或不是由 if 引导的条件从句中，我们也常使用部分倒装。例如：

Were you to see her, you might tell her to come to my home.

Had you been here, everything would have been all right.

在由否定词如 never, nothing, not, seldom, little, hardly, nowhere 等词或 only, so, as 等单词开始的句子或从句中，通常也要使用部分倒装。例如：

Never did I see the like.

Little did Jane think that she was never to see Rochester again.

Not only do lies not provide the "help" hoped for by advocates of benevolent deception; they invade the autonomy of patients and render them unable to make informed choices concerning their own health, including the choice of whether to be a patient in the first place.

Only when he has lost his way does he realize that he wasn't careful enough to make sure that he really did understand.

The Chinese had trained messengers on horseback and runners before 1100 B. C. , as did the ancient Greeks and Romans.

So impressive was this invention, so difficult was it to exceed this speed limit, that nearly 3500 years later, when the first mail coach began operating in England in 1784, it averaged a mere ten mph.

在以 there 开始的句子中,通常会出现完全倒装的句式。例如:

There cannot be more than a dozen students who know of that.

By and by there came a rumor that he had been the King of a distant country.

另外,在一些祈使句和感叹句中也会出现倒装的句式。尤其在记叙文和小说中,为了生动形象地表达句子,以副词开始的感叹句常用完全倒装。但当主语是人称代词时,则人称代词仍然放在动词的前面,构成部分倒装。例如:

Away went the president to the airport.

Off she goes.

Down came the "White Only" notices in buses, hotels, trains, restaurants, sporting events, rest rooms and on park benches that once could be found everywhere throughout the South.

Don't you believe him!

(三)强调句式

在英语文章中,作者为了突出某些重点信息,常会用到强调句式。强调句式包括两类:一种是用助动词 do,does 和 did,将它们放在需强调的实义动词之前,用以强调句子中的谓语。例如:

I did do my homework yesterday evening.

They do have sufficient food and drink.

Ann does have regard for other classmates.

第二种强调句型主要用于强调主语、宾语或状语,被强调的可以是人、物、时间、地点、原因、方式等内容。句式结构是 it is(was)… that (who,which,whom)… 。在此句型中,that 可以用来强调任何主语、宾语或状语。who,whom 只能用来强调人或有生命的东西。which 只能用来强调物或无生命的东西。在这个强调句中,不可以用 where,when,why 等其他单词来强调地点、时间、原因等内容。要想强调这些内容的话,必须用 that。例如:

It was two college students who (that) assisted the blind man cross the street.

It was me whom (that) he sent a New Year card to.

It was light pink that Cathy painted her bedroom.

It was not until he got a map that he started on his way.

It is in the street that I saw an old friend yesterday.

第三节 英语阅读与篇章知识

一、语篇与语篇分析

(一)语篇分析

宏观分析指语篇宏观结构、语篇与外界因素、语篇整体功能等涉及语篇全局特点的研究。语篇宏观结构所反映的是语篇以何种方式组合而成,即语篇表层及底层的架构如何,由何种构件参与语篇架构的形成及语篇内容的完善,由何种语言要素实现语篇的建构等。语篇外界因素指社会因素、认知因素、环境因素等,这些因素对语篇产生影响,属于语篇分析的研究范畴。语篇在社会生活中实现一定的功能,语篇功能的确定主要与语篇的种类和宏观结构或宏观要素相关,因此需要在语篇的宏观层次考察。语篇功能研究与语篇的社会因素分析具有关联,但二者并不等同。前者的研究重点在于功能,而后者的重点在于语篇与社会的联系。①

微观分析指有关语篇基本成分和要素的研究,包括语言成分分析、语篇构成成分分析、语篇所涉及基本要素分析等。微观分析主要关注语篇局部的特点,虽然受制于语篇的宏观框架,但并不深究宏观框架的影响作用。作为语篇内容的基本载体,各种语言成分均有机会参与语篇建构,语言成分间相互关系复杂,对于语篇的影响难以概括,因此具有充分的研究空间。语篇构成成分指按照语篇分析需求而命名的语篇不同层次的单位。其中一些语篇成分常与相应的语言成分同名,如词、句、段等,但作为语篇构成成分使用时,具有与语言成分不同的意义。

(二)英语阅读中的篇章结构

篇章结构是文章学研究的主要对象之一,在其他领域也十分重要,如语法学、文体学、体裁分析等。篇章结构是讲话人或作者有效组织内容所用的谋篇布局的整体结构,该结构也与一定的功能具有密切联系。

语言结构是指从语言角度看待语篇的组织,注重语篇结构在语言上的表现,如句子内部结构、句子之间的衔接、词汇复现、段落之间的过渡、语篇的前后照应等。语篇的语言结构研究主要以语法学研究为基础,语法学研究对语篇宏观结构触及较少,但在微观结构对语篇构件的分析深入、具体。

二、英语阅读与语篇语境理论

语篇中的某个句子与它前面句子之间可能存在句法和语义关系,但这一条件不能完全界定总体连贯语篇。也就是说,每一个句子都可能给前面的句子提供更多的信息。然而,这样的话语有可能不具有可接受性。句子(或话语)的扩展必须构建在宏观结构之下。也就是说,每一个句子从功能上来说必须依赖于至少一个宏观范畴。例如,事件或行为或地点等。因此,句子的每一个语义表达都与某个宏观概念有联系,这不仅是认知过程的一个事实,也是话语本身的一个特性。

---

① 丁维莉,陈维昌,车竞. 篇章理论与英语阅读教学[M]. 北京:世界图书出版公司,2009.

某一个话语具有可接受性,当且仅当这个话语的宏观结构满足一定的进一步描述的条件。例如,对叙事性话语的理论研究和实证研究语篇二者都会首先建立宏观概念,会使用 introduction, complication, resolution 及 concision 等词汇进行引导。在传统的修辞学中也有类似范畴的论述。

语法对不具备可接受性的语篇进行限制,是由于它们违反了宏观结构的条件,请看下列会话:

(1) A: Did you hear about the bank robbery?

B: No. What happened?

A: Yesterday morning I was at our bank round the comer. Suddenly, one of the clients took a gun out of his pocket. He shot a couple of times and then aimed at the cashier. He said that he wanted all the cash she had in her desk. She was very frightened and gave it to him. Then he ran away. The police have not yet caught him.

(2) Suddenly, one of the clients took a gun out of his pocket. She was very frightened and gave it to him. The police have not yet caught him. Yesterday morning I was at our bank round the comer…

(3) Yesterday morning I was at our bank round the comer. The bank is a terrible building. The buildings in this part of town are horrible. But I like living there. The town has no industry. My brother works in a factory. His boss is a terrible guy. He was born in New York in 1909. At that time you could still live in the city (…)

直觉来看,我们发现例(1)是可接受的会话(除了一些口头语的文体因素以外),A 的叙述具有可接受性。但在话语(2)中,该叙述的句子顺序被改变了,明显使话语不仅在语义层面上不符合语法(如缺乏连续性),而且不可接受,其线性指称关系被打乱了。话语(3)满足了线性连贯的条件,每一句与其前句之间都具有语义关系。但我们仍然几乎无法认为它具有可接受性;其中没有"点""线"和"主题",也许可以认为它具有"病态"特征;换言之,此语篇没有宏观结构对其中每一句进行解释。可以对其中的句子进行解释的微观模式关系存在,但被彻底拆散了。话语(3)至多只是对一个非正式谈话的话题的集合。在语法可能确定宏观结构条件的情况下,就能看出(1)和(3)在可接受性上的差别。

值得注意的是,宏观结构可能具有直接的"语言"关联:在(1)中,A

的疑问是关于银行劫案的,他的叙述也与劫案有关联。"劫案"这一词本身没有出现在叙述之中,但 B 仍然知道 A 的问题的命题和他们叙述的对象是同一的,都可以描述为(Yesterday)(ROB)(somebody)(our)(BANK)的某一事件。因此,宏观结构可以直接用这样的表层结构来表达。宏观语义学需要表明这种句子与其语篇的总体意义之间的具体关系。这一关系的存在还可以从另一个角度来推论:如有 The bank was not robbed 这样的句子,与整篇叙述的情况不一致。这种不一致只能在句子与语篇所包含的宏观前提下进行理解。换言之,语篇的句群描述"银行被劫了",即使语法中的一个成分与这个宏观意义不一致,也可以用语篇语法来解释。从实际的状况来看,本族语者一般都能凭直觉,根据上下文来判断语篇的总体意义。识别(1)这种会话的内在关系,删除某个句子与整个语篇之间的不一致,这便是人类认知能力的一部分。

第三章　英语阅读教学设计概述

在英语阅读教学过程中,想要顺利实现教学目标,就需要进行一定的教学设计,合理的教学设计有助于引导学生积极参与到阅读学习中,从而提高自身的阅读能力。本章主要研究英语阅读教学设计的相关知识。

第一节　英语阅读教学活动设计的必要性

一、阅读理解活动层次不够、活动形式单一

就阅读理解活动形式而言,教材中最常用的阅读活动为选择填空和回答问题,其次是讨论和完形填空,其他采用的活动形式有判断正误、匹配、完成句子、翻译、图表填充、角色扮演和复述等。但是,没有信息运用性活动,不管是事实信息还是观点信息,没有评价型活动、综合型活动和创造型活动。虽然讨论可以涉及信息的运用和评价,复述可以涉及综合,但是这些活动形式本身不属于运用、综合、评价或创造型活动。因此,这些活动只能培养学生的信息辨认能力和信息提取能力、信息转述能力和逻辑分析能力,但不能培养学生的运用能力、综合能力和创新能力,更不能培养学生的问题解决能力。缺乏语言的运用,缺乏信息的运用,缺乏观点的运用,缺乏策略和技能的运用,学生的阅读理解能力培养目标则难以达成。

虽然总体阅读理解活动形式相对丰富,但是就一篇阅读来说,形式

第三章　英语阅读教学设计概述

却过于单一,并且只有两三个活动,有些阅读材料只有一个活动。一篇阅读之后,学生只需要解答选择填空或者回答问题,学生如何能够通过阅读活动培养阅读理解能力？更何况有的只有阅读文章而没有任何阅读活动。

教材处理同一类阅读问题时采用的活动形式也过于形式化。难句理解能力的培养方式很多,而《精读》中的 Reading Activity 却采用统一的翻译方式。翻译可以反映一个人对句子的理解程度,但并不是最佳方式,更不是唯一的方式。

从活动使用的频率来看,选择填空、回答问题是每套教材都采用的活动,其次是讨论和完形填空。选择填空可以检测学生的理解,包括信息识别、观点态度理解和推理判断,但是由于其更像测试,课堂教学也就没有了阅读活动。完形填空可以训练学生的逻辑,但是大部分教材的完形填空都是课文的概述,学生根据课文的理解提取信息完成短文填充,检查的是学生对课文内容的掌握。① 作为最常用的活动形式,回答问题本来无可非议,但是由于教材中的问题比较多,各种层次的问题混杂在一起,有理解,有信息识别,还可能有逻辑判断、观点推理等,不利于教学活动的开展。其他活动形式,如复述、背诵不过是最基本的信息转述,虽然是学习的方法之一,但是只能培养最低层次的认知能力,难以满足大学英语教学的要求。

二、活动设计难以保证技能训练

阅读策略和阅读技能的培养是阅读理解教学十分重要的一个目标。策略是一种有意识应用的方式和技巧,而技能则表示学生可以达到自主地使用适当的策略或技巧完成各种阅读任务的程度。

不同的教材,其阅读技能培养的处理方式不同。多数教材没有专项阅读策略教学活动,而是希望通过常规的阅读活动培养学生的阅读技能。但是,选择填空、判断正误甚至是完成句子、完形填空、翻译和匹配,都难以培养学生的阅读策略。

教学活动的设计决定着教材是否可以实施课程目标,教材是学生学

---

① 王笃勤. 大学英语阅读教学活动设计[M]. 哈尔滨:哈尔滨工程大学出版社,2011.

习的主要媒介,更是教师教学的主要工具,教学活动的设计必须适应学生的认知特征,符合学生的认知规律,必须有利于教学的开展。阅读作为一种认知活动不只是表现为知识和领会两个层次,同样包含分析、综合、评价、运用等层次。目前大学英语阅读教材的编写在活动设计方面仍旧存在很多问题,教材在活动编写中忽略了阅读的认知需求,缺乏综合、评价、创造型和运用型活动,难以培养学生的阅读技能和语言运用能力,这也就给大学英语教师开展阅读教学提出了更大的挑战,教师必须根据学生的需求设计能够培养各层次能力的阅读活动。

第二节 英语阅读准备活动设计

一、阅读准备活动

阅读准备活动,是指在学生阅读文本之前开展的活动。阅读准备活动有助于学生做好语言准备,预热文本的话题,并激活学生原有的知识,是阅读过程中必不可少的环节。研究表明,准备活动有助于学生获得文本背景知识,提供理解文本所必需的特定信息,激发读者兴趣,在学生头脑中构成对文本的预测,并且帮助学生选择适合该文本的阅读策略,加深对文本的理解,同时减轻了阅读难度。根据阅读准备的内容,阅读前准备活动可分为心理准备、语言准备和图式准备。

(一)心理准备

1. 心理准备的内涵

所谓心理准备,指学生在阅读前是否拥有阅读的欲望、需求,是否对即将阅读的材料感兴趣,是否具有较强的阅读动机。从教学设计的角度出发,心理准备活动也因此指帮助学生从心理、情感和态度等方面做好阅读的准备。

第三章 英语阅读教学设计概述

研究表明,心理因素是影响阅读的主要因素。当学生缺乏阅读兴趣、缺乏阅读的需求时,其理解就会受阻。阅读教学也因此必须高扬积极的心理因素,激发对阅读材料的积极心理,消除消极因素,克服焦虑心理,帮助学生从思想上对即将进行的阅读活动做好准备,产生阅读动机。

阅读中的情感,包括学习者的态度、动机、个性、焦虑、移情、抑制、自信心和学习风格等,可以促进理解,也可能影响理解;可以促进记忆,也可能给记忆带来混乱;可以反馈记忆内容,带来学习动力,也可以说情感是有效利用已有资源的前提。

二语习得的相关研究,尤其是克拉申(Krashen)的情感过滤假说,也都证明情感因素在学习中的作用。情感可使学习者产生某种倾向或爱好,消极情感可导致抵制,而积极情感为学习开通道路。情感屏障妨碍着语言习得者充分利用可理解输入,当情感屏障强时,习得者也可能听懂或读懂语言输入,但输入到达不了语言习得机制。阅读是一种输入性活动,如果不能激发积极的情感因素,如自尊自信、移情、动机、愉快和惊喜,一些消极因素,如害怕、羞涩、紧张、沮丧,就会占据学习者的心理,从而影响阅读的开展。事实证明,兴趣是积极探索或从事某项活动的认识或意识倾向,是引起学生学习动机、推动学生主动学习的一种重要心理因素。

2. 心理准备活动的功能

(1)激发阅读动机

动机是一种非智力因素,是学习者学习的内部动力。阅读共有三种动机:寻求乐趣、深入理解和获取信息。然而,在教学实践中,教师往往忽略阅读动机的激发,很多学生因为对教材不感兴趣,看不到阅读的必要性,感受不到阅读的意义,所以表现很懈怠,甚至不参与课堂活动。心理准备可以通过提问、相关背景介绍、欲望制造和有用性联想等方式帮助学生认识阅读的必要性、有用性、趣味性,激发其阅读的动机和渴望,使其对即将阅读的材料产生积极的心理反应。

(2)集中关注、启动阅读

没有阅读目标的活动没有真正的学习价值,目标决定了学生采取的阅读策略以及阅读后所记忆的内容,具备明确的阅读目标便于进一步理解文章内外的信息。课堂阅读所选择的材料与日常的个性化阅读材料不同,不能根据自己的兴趣爱好、阅读目的去关注和研究文本的相关内容。根据学生的学习阶段不同,教师可以有计划地设计不同的培养目标,同一篇文章在学习的初期或许只要求学生能够寻找必要的信息,而到了高级阶段或许要求阅读者关注体裁、主旨(文章表现了什么思想,抒发了什么感情)、层次(文章分为哪几层,从哪几个方面来写人记事、表情达意)、写法(文章主要运用了什么写作方法,语言有什么特点)、重要语句(哪些语句与中心事件、中心人物和中心思想有密切关系)。因此,心理准备活动将有助于集中阅读者的关注力,并让他们对未来的训练目标有一个清晰的概念。

同时,阅读准备有助于阅读者行之有效地寻找信息。心理准备活动有助于集中阅读者的关注力,让他们有的放矢地进行阅读活动。例如,在阅读一篇关于西方餐桌礼仪的文章时,首先根据文章的顺序准备一些问题,有的放矢的阅读会减轻阅读活动的强度,把阅读者的视线牵引到某些必需的细节或关注点上,而非巨细无遗地阅读。以往很多失败的阅读活动大多与阅读者期望能够把每个字句都完全理解甚至翻译过来有关系。阅读者可以在具有内在逻辑的若干问题的引导下对全文产生进行系统性认识,信息搜索也将因此更有效率。

(二)语言准备

语言能力是英语阅读最基础的支柱,是影响二语阅读的关键因素。尽管"自上而下"的理论强调图式的重要性,但是研究表明,当语言能力达不到应有的水平时,学生的相关图式无法补充其语言的不足。而当学生的二语水平达到其"门槛"要求,其母语阅读能力就可以迁移到外语阅读中来。由此来看,语言能力是阅读的基础,如果学生当下的语言能力有可能影响其阅读,如果文本中的语言现象影响其理解,那么就有必要做适当的语言准备。

1. 句法功能的准备

从语言的基本功能角度上看,语言具有寒暄功能(phatic function)、指令功能(directive)、信息功能(informative)、疑问功能(interrogative)、表达功能(expressive)、表情功能(evocative)、言语行为功能(performative)。

第三章 英语阅读教学设计概述

如果学生不了解语言的基本功能就会给阅读造成困难。例如《大学英语》第二册 Lessons from Jefferson 一课，教师提出问题"What did Jeffereon do?"要求学生在阅读中寻找杰斐逊在处理问题时采取的行为方式。但学生对句子的表意功能掌握不够，有的学生甚至将"Jefferson was for many years the object of strong criticism. I steer my ship with hope, leaving fear behind"作为答案。显然是学生不理解被动态用于表达遭遇，而"I steer my ship with hope, leaving fear behind"这样的比喻性的句子表达感情和态度，不是表达一个人的行为，从而导致理解错误。由此来看，教学设计要根据学生的不同语言基础作不同的语言准备。

2. 语句逻辑的准备

学生要理解文本的逻辑就必须具有一定的逻辑基础。在大学阶段，当我们说到语句逻辑时，教师们一般会关注比较隐性的语句表达，而不是这里所说的通过连词表达的逻辑。因为一般情况下，这种语言知识是不需要准备的。如果需要准备，我们一般会选择在中学可能没有接触过的逻辑表达。其实，更需要准备的是独立单句之间的逻辑关系。例如 as，多数学生对这个词汇的理解为：连词，表达因果关系。然而事实上这个词汇在作连词的时候至少具有三种逻辑可能，要根据语境来判断。例如：

You will grow wiser as you grow older.（两动作同时进行）

As rain has fallen, the air is cooler.（因果关系）

Strange as it may seem, nobody was injured in the accident.（让步关系，等于 though）

这三个例句所带有的逻辑关系在中学时期都有涉及，但是学生在运用时难免出现问题。教师可以有意在阅读前进行梳理，列举简单的语句要求学生判断其逻辑类型，而后在文中遇到相应的语句时再特别设计问题，看学生是否能判断出答案的位置。

句子内部和外部的逻辑可以用连词、从句、分句、伴随状态、介词短语来表达。段落间和篇章整体过渡的逻辑依赖连词和过渡句。连词在高中时期就进行过比较系统的介绍，词义也比较具体明确，大学阶段只要继续积累就可以了。而比较复杂的从句和伴随状态则具有多种可能性，可以是表达因果关系的状语，表达两动作同时进行或表达条件关系的状语等。例如,下面是典型的伴随状态的句子。

And most of all, he bought the run-down Gordon Arms Hotel and totally restored it, transforming it from a mess into a glorious first-class hotel with 30 handsomely furnished rooms, wood-paneled stairs, false bookshelves with fake leather books and an outstanding restaurant.

本例选自《新视野大学英语》第三册第一单元,现在分词作结果状语,详细解释了restore的结果。事实上,学生对因果关系中的因更加熟悉,而对于表结果的情况相对生疏,因此提前导入非常必要。再如:

Mr. Abdy, a 27-year-old businessman, acquired the bulk of the properties for about half a million pounds, obtaining bank loans and striking deals with various people to pay only a part of what they are owed by Mr. Williams.

本例选自《新视野大学英语》第三册第一单元,现在分词作方式状语,解释主语是通过怎样的手段达到acquired the bulk of properties的目的。在教学中,教师可就这两个句子提出细节问题,考查学生是否具备相关的逻辑意识,如果学生缺乏相应的语法意识,建议做适当的处理。

    3. 语词和抽象概念的准备

在阅读某些篇章时,虽然会碰到一定数量的生疏单词,但借助读者对词根、词缀的了解可以对词汇有大概的了解,再配合上下文,读者可以猜测出它们的意义。影响阅读的往往是无法根据语境推测出来的词汇和概念。同时有些概念比较抽象,即便提供了相应的中文译名,学生依旧无法推知概念的内涵,类似的专业性强、脱离普通学生生活经历的概念就必须在阅读前导入。

二、阅读准备活动的设计

(一)教材本位法

随着大学英语教学理论研究的进展以及现代教育技术的日新月异,各类教材丰富了大学英语课堂,给师生带来更多的选择。比如《大学英语》第三版教材,选材多为名篇,语言美好,句型结构类型丰富,内涵跨度

第三章　英语阅读教学设计概述

大。选篇中各种文体类型均有,但是应用文基本上没有涉及。第一、二册和第三、四册之间的语言难度差异非常大,理解能力和分析能力较差的学生往往在进入三级阅读时感到有困难。阅读前需要教师设计相应的语言和图示准备活动。

另外,教材一般都为教师提供了一定量的读前准备材料,如课文正文之前一般都有 lead-in question,这些问题大多是根据文章话题设计的,和文章的吻合度非常高,教师可以参照使用;课文正文之前多有综述段,大多只有一两句话,却能一定程度上揭示文章的主旨或主要人物事迹,可以利用这些简短的表述进行文章内容预测;各教材配套电子教案中的音、视频材料大多是真实生活的片段或从影视作品中剪辑下来的,内容多涉及课文文化背景,可以借助它们丰富文化导入;电子教案和教参书中一般都有作者介绍,尤其是小说类作品必须预先介绍作家的写作风格和生平,学生才能深入理解文章的内涵,而不至于流于表面;各教材都配套设计了网络学习资源,教师同样可以根据网络资源给学生布置比较耗费时间的准备活动,比如同类文章,进行阅读前心理准备和核心概念的语言准备。

(二)话题本位法

每一个单元都会有独特的话题,学生的先在经验和知识受生活经验和学习经验的制约,对各种话题的了解程度也往往大相径庭。为此,教师应当针对不同的话题,采用不同的准备活动。例如,记叙文一般都有比较完整的情节、鲜活的人物性格塑造、深刻的写作主旨,只要让学生对即将阅读的材料做足心理准备,就容易激发学生对阅读的兴趣。因此,可以采用标题预测、热身问题讨论等形式,让学生对阅读材料的内容进行预测。之后在阅读过程中,必然有许多新信息出乎学生的意料,在学生的脑海中形成刺激性的标示记忆,有助于阅读理解和分析的进行。又如论证型文章,大多讨论的是类似环保、节能、克隆技术、大学生活和就业压力,话题比较严肃,阅读过程中容易产生沉重感。[①] 同时这些话题的作品句型也通常比较复杂,单词更书面化、术语频繁出现、篇章逻辑性非常严谨,语言形式难度比较大。因此在处理类似的文章时,就必须预

[①] 汪艳萍. 英语阅读教学与写作研究[M]. 北京:世界图书出版公司,2017.

先对相关的核心词汇做语言准备,如头脑风暴,使学生对阅读材料中的核心词、术语概念及其之间的意义联系有比较丰满的认识。热点话题大多也是社会媒体关注的核心,剪辑一段新闻、影片、音乐都可以形象地带入关键话题的概念,活跃课堂,缓解沉重感。

第三种常见的文体是说明文,可以分为说理说明文和事物说明文两种。直观的图片或实物配合上讨论或图表对比型的活动会非常适合。例如《大学体验英语》第三册 Sources of Information 完全可以模拟旅游咨询,让学生集体提供建议:我准备去印度旅行,请问可以从哪里获得必要的信息。而后将学生的建议以表格形式都列举在黑板上,再请学生对各种信息来源进行评述,讨论它们的优势和不足。

第三节　英语知识与领会活动设计

一、知识与领会的表现形式

(一)知识类活动

阅读理解是阅读者从自己的一般知识和语篇的明示性陈述中获得信息的过程。它实际上是一种通过书面语言完成的交际活动。在阅读理解的过程中,阅读者的目的是获取阅读信息,为此,阅读者通常要在一定知识的基础上采用一定的阅读策略,在作者、读者以及文本之间建立某种模式,从而使语篇基础与情境模式相互关联并形成交际情景。在这种交际模式下,阅读者才能真正从阅读文本中获取阅读信息,并充分理解作者所要表达的真实意图和内在情感。但是,就理解而言,却包含不同的认知层次,其中知识和领会是两个最基本的层次。那么,什么是知识?什么是领会?领会的知识层次与一般概念上的知识又有什么不同呢?

第三章　英语阅读教学设计概述

1. 知识和知识类活动

在大学英语教学活动中,知识类活动设计是最基础最低层次的教学活动。那么,如何定义知识和知识类活动呢？一般概念上的知识指可以转述的各种信息,而阅读理解中的知识却不是信息本身,而是理解的一种表现形式。根据布卢姆教育目标分类学对认知层次的分类,"知识表现为对所学知识的识别、回忆,属于低层次的认知能力。就英语学习而言,词汇意思和语法结构的再认以及对话和课文复述等都属于知识层次"。那么阅读理解中知识类活动就是指信息的再认和重复。知识类活动虽然未必是对信息内涵的真正理解,却是阅读者进行进一步的理解、分析、综合、评价和应用的基础。

2. 知识类活动的表现形式

在实际教学活动中,以下均可以被认定为知识类的活动。
(1) 识别并复述阅读文本中显性细节

所谓显性细节,指文本中有语言明确表达的信息,亦即文本的字面所表达的内容。例如,在《大学英语》(第三版)第三册第三单元 *Why I Teach* 的教学活动中,找出"the names of his students that offer the reasons why the author Peter G. Beidler teaches"的活动就是知识类活动。阅读者快速阅读课文,在一分钟之内就能够找到这个问题的答案。"Vicky, George, Jeanne and Jacqui are the names of his students that offer the reasons why the author Peter G. Beidler teaches",这就是典型的识别阅读文本中显性细节的活动。

(2) 按显性顺序识别并转述阅读文本中的事件、方式、要点等

对事件顺序的识别,对说明文中细节的转述也属于知识类活动。如在《大学英语》(第三版)第三册第三单元 *Why I Teach* 的教学中,要求阅读者在5分钟之内找到"the author's reasons for choosing teaching as his career",大部分阅读者都能在规定时间内识别文章第5—9段段首句中的信息点,以及17—21段中相应的信息点是作者选择教书作为终身职业的原因,并简单地罗列出以下内容。

—the pace of the academic calendar
—variety (teaching is built on change)

—the freedom to be his own boss (the freedom to do things his own way)

—the opportunity to keep on learning

—the opportunity to teach his students to play their roles in the real world

—the opportunity to share with his students the happiness of their success

—the joy of seeing his students grow and change in front of his eyes

—the power to help his students grow and change

—the love teaching offers, the love of learning, of books and ideas and the love a teacher feels for rare students

—the feeling of remaining young while teaching

再如图表填充活动,如果要求填写的内容为事实信息,也应该归为知识类活动。但是,由于不是知识的再认,而是转述,对学生的语言表达能力有一定的要求,难度高于识别,但是所有的学生都应该达到最基本的目标。例如:

- Activity 1

Work on the author's personal file.

Step 1 Assign the learning task.

Work individually to finish the following personal file for the author.

When did he want to become a writer?

When did the possibility take hold?

①What assignment did his English teacher give?

②What did he do with it at first?

How did the possibility take hold?

③What topic did he choose?

④What did the teacher do with his essay?

Step 2 Students work individually on the file.

Step 3 Students work in pairs to compare their work.

Step 4 Call on an individual pair for feedback.

When did he want to become a writer?

Since his childhood in Belleville.

When did the possibility take hold?

Not until his third year in high school.

①What assignment did his English teacher give?

The teacher assigned several topics for them to choose for wanting of informal essays.

②What did he do with it at first?

He was not willing to write at first and delayed until the night.

③What topic did he choose?

The Art of Eating Spaghetti.

④What did the teacher do with his essay?

The teacher read his essay to the class and pronounced it as having grasped the essence of the essay.

(二)领会活动

1. 领会类活动与知识类活动的区别

领会表现为"转化""解释"和"推断领会"的表达方式,包括阅读后选择适当的图片、推断说话者的意图、谈话的主题、预测故事的发展等。那么如何定义"转化""解释"和"推断"呢?"转化"包括把文本形式转化为符号形式,如把文本转化为图解、地图、表格、图表、曲线图以及数学公式等;或者把一些非逐字逐句的表述,如隐喻、象征手法、反语、夸张转化为普通语言。这些都属于领会的范畴。

语言信息的直接转述未必表示领会,可能是鹦鹉学舌,而图片、动作的信息转化则代表读者对信息所指的理解。能够转述"It is cold here.",不过是信息转述,而能够推断说话者暗含的"Please close the window."的请求才是真实的理解。大学阶段的阅读教学必须侧重学生理解能力的培养,而不只是信息的转述、再认。

2. 领会理解的内容

(1)基本事实信息的理解

这里是指读者能在识别(文本、图片和行为)、转述或复述文本相关显性细节的基础上对这些信息进行进一步的排序、演示或者图解。与知识类活动不同,领会类活动不仅仅是阅读者对阅读文本中显性细节和显性顺序的识别和回忆,还应包括阅读者对基本事实信息的再加工。下面的活动通过学生的解释训练学生的理解能力,不仅可以训练学生对具体表述的理解,同样可以训练学生对上下文的理解。

- Activity (《新版大学英语综合教程》第一册 Unit 1)

Explain the followings.

Step 1 Assign the learning task.

Work in pairs to discuss how you can explain the followings.

①Why Baker anticipated another cheerless year?

②Why Baker prepared for discipline?

③What kinds of assignments were dull and difficult?

Step 2 Students work in pairs to discuss their understandings.

Step 3 Call on an individual pair to answer.

①学生可以通过下文对 Mr. Fleagle 的介绍了解为什么作者有此预测,解释时自然是利用下文信息。从表达逻辑上也是下文解释前面的陈述。

②对此的解释需要学生借助课文中 36 行至 37 行 to write it as I wanted, however, would violate all the rules of formal composition, 而通过这个信息学生也可以理解 discipline 为 punishment。

③从 line 4 "I hated the assignments to turn out to be long, lifeless paragraphs that were agony for teachers to read and for me to write." 可以推断什么样是最乏味的。

(2)观点态度信息的理解

观点态度包括文本中显性表达的观点态度和需要读者推理判断的隐含的观点态度,可以是说明议论中例证说明的观点,可以是说话语义中转达的态度,亦可以是行为表现的观点态度。观点态度的理解不只是能识别表述作者的观点,同时还包括能找到支持作者观点态度的信息,或用自己的语言解释作者的观点的信息。下面的活动就是先给出推断,让学生通过阅读理解寻找可以解释这个推断的证据。

- Activity (《新版大学英语综合教程》第一册 Unit 1)

Find evidence for the followings.

Step 1 Assign the learning task.

Work in groups of four to find evidence for the followings.

①Baker was unwilling to write the essay at first.

②All the English courses were dull.

③The author's expectation was right.

④Baker had a strong desire to write for himself.

⑤Baker had thought he would be punished for not having submitted an essay as required.

Step 2 Students work individually.

Step 3 Students work in groups to share their work with each other.

Step 4 Call on an individual pair for feedback.

参考答案：

①line 20. I took the list home and did nothing until the night before the essay was due. Lying on the sofa, I finally faced up to the unwelcome task, took the list out of my notebook, and scanned it.

②line 7. When our class was assigned to Mr. Fleagle for a third-year English I anticipated another cheerless year in that most tedious subjects.

③line 16. I prepared for an unfruitful year with Mr. Fleagle and for a long time was not disappointed.

④Paragraph 5. Suddenly I wanted to write about that, about the warmth and good feeling of it, but I wanted to put it down simply for my own joy, not for Mr. Fleagle.

⑤line 44. I was preparing myself for a command to report to Mr. Fleagle immediately after school for discipline.

(3)大意主题的理解

这里的大意主题是指某一阅读材料的中心思想或主题。如果阅读者能在文本中找到、确认或提取其主题句，那么这属于知识类活动的范畴。但是，如果学生需要理解细节与主题之间的关系，根据文章中的具体例证说明文章大意主题则属于领会活动。下面活动要求学生判断相应段落的主题。由于采用匹配的方式，要求相对较低。如果学生水平比较高，可以让学生写出每一段的主题。

- Activity (《新版大学英语综合教程》第一册 Unit 1)

Step 1 Assign the learning task.

Match the following headings with the paragraph numbers.

Baker's sudden desire to write about that topic.

Enjoyment brought by the reading of Baker's essay/Classmates' response to the essay.

Baker's feelings about English courses.

A topic that attracts Baker's attention.

Sweet/vivid memories awaked by the topic.

Mr. Fleagle's announcement.

Anticipating punishment/discipline.

Baker discovered what he wanted to do in life.

Baker's impression of his new English teacher.

Step 2 Students work it individually first then compare their answers in pairs.

Step 3 Call on an individual pair for feedback.

参考答案：

①Baker's feelings about English courses

②Baker's impression of his new English teacher

③A topic that attracts Baker's attention

④Sweet/vivid memories awaked by the topic

⑤Baker's sudden desire to write about that topic

⑥Anticipating punishment/discipline

⑦Mr. Fleagle' announcement

⑧Enjoyment brought by the reading of Baker's essay/Classmates' response to the essay

⑨Baker discovered what he wanted to do in life

（4）文学性欣赏和文化内涵的理解

在大学阶段，阅读理解的教学应该有别于初、高中阶段的教学，侧重于加强有关语言所承载的文化知识的教学，加深学生对文本的文学性和文化内涵的理解。文化内涵的理解属于文本理解的较高层次，要求阅读者在读懂文章的主旨大意等基本内容的基础上，深入理解文字后面隐含的深刻意义。这种活动一般需要教师具备一定的文学素养，课前认真准备，课上由浅入深地指导学生理解文章深意。下面以海明威的一个作品为例阐述文学性欣赏和文化内涵理解的重要性。

美国小说家欧内斯特·海明威（Ernest Hemingway，1899—1961）

第三章　英语阅读教学设计概述

一向以"文坛硬汉"著称,是美利坚民族的精神丰碑,1954年度(第54届)的诺贝尔文学奖获得者、"新闻体"小说的创始人,《大学英语》第三版(精读)第三册第6课 A Day's Wait 就是海明威的作品。在学习这篇文章的时候,教师不仅仅要帮助学生掌握文章的生词、语法、主旨大意、文章结构等基本阅读信息,更应该赏析文章的文化内涵,体会文章的文学性,理解作者所要表达的文学底蕴。

第一,帮助学生理解海明威生平和作品的主题之间的关系。

在 A Day's Wait 这篇文章的阅读活动之初,教师会要求学生快速阅读课文,理解文章中小主人公一整天都在勇敢地等待死亡的来临,而"死亡"和"勇气"正是海明威作品的主题。教师还可以介绍海明威的生平和海明威之死,让学生深入思考"生与死"这个命题。

第二,引导学生理解文中为什么增加描写主人公的父亲外出打猎的内容。在学习 A Day's Wait 这篇文章时,教师可以特别提醒学生,为什么惜字如金的海明威会用26、27两个段落描写主人公的父亲外出打猎的内容?

- Activity

At first glance, the hunting scene may seem to have little to do with the plot.

1899年7月21日,海明威出生在美国芝加哥的一个医生家庭。幼年起,他就开始跟随父亲钓鱼、打猎、踢球等。海明威的母亲是有着良好艺术修养的教徒,她经常带海明威去参观画展并听音乐会,培养了海明威良好的艺术修养和文学素养。1917年美国对德宣战后,海明威志愿担任战地救护车司机,赴欧洲前线参战,目睹并亲身经历了战争的残酷。第二次世界大战期间,海明威曾作为战地记者到达巴黎前线,并组织过游击队抗击德国法西斯。海明威一生经历过两次世界大战和无数次的生死考验。正是这种经历,让海明威的作品始终围绕着"死亡(death)"和"勇气(courage)"这两个主题。

海明威1961年7月2日选择用猎枪结束自己的生命,他的轻生被认为是不堪忍受各种病痛的长期折磨而做出的选择。有人认为这是他在用死亡维护自己作为人的尊严。也有人称颂这是海明威一贯推崇的充满勇气地平静面对死亡。文中小主人公选择平静、孤独地等待死亡的来临是否正是海明威要表达的:病痛是对生命的凌辱,死亡应该平静面对呢?

However, the author has reasons to describe it. What are the reasons?

通过对文章文化内涵的分析,阅读者渐渐体会到这段打猎的描写有着如下原因。

①It diverts the readers so that the boy's real thoughts will be a greater surprise when they are revealed.

②It creates a sense of time passing so that we know it is close to evening by the time the father gets home.

③It brings out a contrast between the father's robust activities outside and the boy's terrible tension inside.

通过阅读打猎这个段落,阅读者可以体会海明威作为"迷惘"中走出的"硬汉"在作品中不间断地进行"硬汉式"的探索,始终抱有希望,永不放弃,永不言败。也让阅读者进一步理解海明威的那句名言:"Man is not made for defeat. A man can be destroyed but not defeated. (人并非为败而生。人可以被消灭,但不能被击败。)"海明威被称为"迷惘的一代"的代表。在海明威的作品中,我们不难体会一种世事无常的悲哀和悲观厌世的态度。但是,我们又能在他的作品中发现他对不完美人生中自我救赎的追求,这就是所谓的"硬汉"精神。

第三,帮助学生理解海明威小说的写作风格。教师可以设计一个教学活动,让学生自己分析海明威的写作风格。

• Activity

Read the text carefully and find evidence which shows the author's writing style as listed in the left column. 1

What's the matter, Schatz?

I've got a headache.

Economical and Effective Dialogue

You'd better go back to bed.

No, I'm all right.

You can't come in, he said.

Short Sentences. Simple Words

You mustn't get what I've got.

这个教学活动可以帮助学生理解海明威的小说在文字方面有着自己独特的风格,用词准确、简单、含蓄,对20世纪欧美文学创作有着重大的影响。海明威被称为新闻体小说的开创者,而他的写作风格是典型的现代叙事风格。

第四,帮助学生理解课文中用词的深刻含义。*A Day's Wait* 这篇文章内容并不复杂,讲的是一个九岁的男孩因为不了解 Fahrenheit 和 Celsius 两种不同温度计量单位的区别,误以为发热华氏 102 度的自己即将面临死亡,他因此选择孤独、平静地等待这一刻的来临。而 Fahrenheit 和 Celsius 两种计量单位隐含的意思是什么呢? Fahrenheit 和 Celsius 是两种看待世界的价值观,用不同的价值观来看待同样的问题会得出完全不同的结论,会影响一个人对事物的判断,甚至会造就一个人截然不同的命运。

故事的缘起是孩子对体温的误解,但是文中的误解又何止于此? 儿子和父亲之间也充满误解,起初父亲不了解儿子独自面对死亡的绝望,而阴霾过后的第二天,父亲依然不理解儿子的内心。海明威虽然用词简单,但是他所要表达的意义是深刻的。这就可以解释为什么海明威总是不停地修改自己的手稿,直到发表前一天。对于这种用词用句有着深刻内涵的文章,教师经常需要帮助阅读者"推断"或推理性理解文章字面意义之外的深刻含义。

二、知识与领会活动的设计

(一)知识类活动的设计

1. 根据学生理解需求设计知识类活动

本课题的项目研究显示,预备级学生由于语言基础较差,词汇量不够,缺乏应有的句法意识,很多时候连字面意思理解都有困难,知识类活动对这些学生来说是必不可少的。下面的知识类活动要求学生能够完成故事的事实信息填空,是比较常用的一种活动形式。由于要求填写的都是故事中的具体事实信息,所填写内容没有变化性,不需要学生重新组织语言,活动也因此要求比较低,是所有学生都必须达到的目标。

• Activity(《新版大学英语综合教程》第一册 Unit 1)

Getting to know the story.

Step 1 Assign the learning task.

Work individually to complete the following sentences to complete the whole story about the author.

(1) Baker had wished to _____ ever since childhood in Belleville.

(2) However, the English courses had always seemed _____ and he _____ writing, so this idea seemed _____ for him until _____ .

(3) His class was assigned to _____ that year, who was famous for _____ . For a long time, _____ changed.

(4) Later in the year, when they began their _____ lessons, the teacher gave them a list of topics to choose from.

(5) It was a long difficult decision as almost all seemed _____ . When at the last minute his eye stopped on _____ .

(6) The topic reminded him of _____ when Baker and his family tried spaghetti for supper.

(7) To _____ , he took up his pen and began to write but he had no more time for write another respectable one for Mr. Fleagle when he finished and had to turn in _____ .

(8) In class, when everyone's paper was returned, he was waiting for the teacher _____ .

(9) However, the teacher read his essay to the class, and everyone _____ .

(10) When Mr. Fleagle announced his writing reflected _____ and _____ him, Baker, for the first time, got acknowledged and assured, and in this eleventh grade, he _____ .

Step 2 Students work individually on the sentence completion.

Step 3 Students work in pairs to check their understanding.

参考答案：

(1) become a writer

(2) dull, hated, impossible, the third year in high school

(3) Mr. Fleagle, dullness and inability to inspire, nothing

(4) informal writing

(5) dull, The Art of Eating Spaghetti

第三章 英语阅读教学设计概述

(6) sweet/vivid/happy memories

(7) relive the pleasure, his tale of the Belleville supper

(8) criticize/scold him

(9) laughed/was filled with open-hearted enjoyment

(10) essence of writing, congratulated, discovered what he wished to do in life

2. 根据教材理解的需要设计知识类活动

材料不同,知识类活动表现形式也不同,具体的知识包括术语的知识和具体事实的知识。术语的知识包括专用术语的特征、属性或关系、词汇的一般意义等。如果学生有限的具体知识造成了对文章理解的困难,就应该依据材料的不同,增加术语知识活动和具体事实知识的活动。[①] 下面活动的目的是辨别有关科技的事实性信息,是最简单的知识目标达成活动,要求学生判断所描述的事实信息在文章中是否提到。

- Activity(《新版大学英语综合教程》第一册 Unit 3)

Recall of information.

Step 1 Assign the learning task.

In this text, Hawking presents some facts about science and different attitudes on the public and the way to educate the public. Now, please read the text and tell which of the following are mentioned in the text.

(1) Even the privileged had no access to modern medicine in the past.

(2) The public is in two minds about science.

(3) Science is often taught in terms of equations in schools.

(4) Hawking's book sold twice as many as others because of Einstein's equation.

(5) Only a small number of people read books.

(6) We have not been contacted by an alien civilization because civilizations tend to destroy themselves when they reach our stage.

Step 2 The teacher read the sentence one by one while the whole class answers the question.

---

① 王丹. 英语阅读教学理论与实践[M]. 北京:知识产权出版社,2018.

3. 增加知识类活动的真实性和趣味性

一般情况下，知识类活动不易激发学生的阅读兴趣。但是，如果能在设计知识类活动时纳入真实性理念，让学生为了一个真实的目的而获取信息，学生阅读的积极性就能大大增强。同时，在教学设计时，应利用图片、实物、视频等增加知识类活动的趣味性。以《大学英语》第三册第 7 单元 1 为例：

- Activity

Talk according to the pictures.
Step 1 Assign the learning task.
Step 2 Students prepare telling the story with the help of the pictures.
Step 3 Group retelling of the story. Students work in groups, each talk about one picture and the others following the former according to the following ones.

本活动要求学生根据图片复述故事，从内容角度来看，学生所做的更多的图片来自《大学英语》第三册第 7 单元电子教案，是事实内容再现，因此属于知识目标活动。虽然这类活动对学生的理解能力、分析能力、综合能力都没有要求，更没有评价的要求，但这是英语语言能力发展的基础。很多时候我们通过提问、选择和匹配等训练了学生的某种了解能力，有时甚至训练了学生的评价能力，但是，如果学生不能转述信息，不能再现文章的信息，那么其语言能力的发展就缺乏应有的基础。活动时最好给学生足够的时间让他们在小组之内练习，保证每个学生都能得到训练。反馈时不要让一名学生完成所有图片的介绍，可以尝试一名学生只做一幅图片的复述，其他学生衔接上一个学生的复述，这样不仅增加了复述的挑战性，同时也可以促进学生的参与。

4. 要适量适度

知识类活动主要体现在阅读者对阅读文本中显性细节的识别和回忆上。在教学设计时，此类活动所占的比例应有所考量，力争适度适量。在阅读者水平低于或与阅读文本难度水准相当的情况下，如果知识类活动设计不足，可能导致阅读者阅读信心受损，影响语篇推理行为，最终使读者与作者之间的书面语言交际受阻。但是，如果此类活动设计过多，也会加重读者的认知负荷,降低读者在阅读过程中的积极主动性,损害阅读者的阅读动机,妨害阅读课程教学目标的达成。

(二)领会活动的设计

1. 内容本位法

阅读理解的活动形式应与其内容相适应,行为的理解、空间的理解其表现形式有所不同,事件发生顺序的理解和写作意图的理解表现形式不同,推理判断也会有不同的表现形式。阅读理解活动的形式也因此会因内容不同而变化。活动1是以《新版大学英语综合教程》第一册 Unit 8 为例所进行的教学设计。活动1要求学生用图表表示文章中介绍的教育变化,将其"转化"为图表进行表达。采用了图表转化的方式。

- Activity 1 Charting education.

Step 1 Assign the learning task.

We can see the role education plays in one's life. Can you draw a chart to show the change of education and profession? You can locate the education level and profession on the chart below.

0＝no education

0.6＝primary education

0.8＝basic education

1.2＝high education

Assign the learning task.

Work in groups of four to find evidence for the following.

(1) Baker was unwilling to write the essay at first.

(2) All the English courses were dull.

(3) The author's expectation was right.

(4) Baker had a strong desire to write for himself.

(5) Baker had thought he would be punished for not having submitted an essay as required.

Students work individually.

Students work in groups to share with work.

Feedback.

2. 循序渐进法

读者对阅读文本的理解是逐步加深的,对信息的认知往往要经历"识别""转述"和"自由表达"等多个阶段,理解类活动应该由浅入深、由易到难、循序渐进地逐层展现。即使同一层次的活动也会涉及控制性表达和自由表达等不同表达形式。一般情况下,输入类活动在前,输出类活动在后,控制性输出在前,非控制性输出在后。教学设计也要尊重阅读者的心理规律,充分考虑理解类活动的序列设计的必要性和重要性。

所谓理解活动的序列,是指在大学英语教学活动中,教师设计的理解活动的先后顺序。由于理解类活动的"转化""解释"和"推断"三个层次是逐层加深的,理解类活动的序列就应该以"转化"为序列的初级,以"解释"为序列的中级,以"推断"为序列的高级。

以《大学英语》第二册第 3 单元为例,下面的理解活动就是按照循序渐进的原则设计的。

- Activity【回答下列问题】

Step 1 Assign the learning task.

(1) How did the author feel about the journey to the interview?

(2) What was his first impression of the school?

(3) What was his first impression of the headmaster?

(4) Why did the headmaster looked at the author with an air of surprised disapproval?

(5) Why did the headmaster grunt twice?

(6) What did the headmaster think of games?

(7) Why did the teaching set-up with him with fear?

(8) Was the author satisfied with the salary?

(9) What did he think of working under a woman?

Step 2 Students work individually.

Step 3 Students work in groups to share with work.

Step 4 Feedback.

参考答案:

(1) He felt the journey was awkward. /He felt depressed/He was

rather annoyed at the journey.

(2) It was simple and surroundings were terrible with dust, fumes and busy traffic.

(3) He looked like a headmaster, which was not so desirable.

(4) Maybe the author was too young, seemingly inexperienced and incompetent for the teaching post. /It was not the type of applicants he had been looking for.

(5) The first time he grunted just to show his helpless acceptance of the unwanted applicant. The second time he grunted to show his disapproval or dissatisfaction with the author's answer.

(6) He thought games were a vital part of a boy's education.

(7) He had to teach at three different levels, he had to teach what he was incompetent at. And what's more, he had to teach when his friends were enjoying their leisure.

(8) No, he was not satisfied to earn so little for such heavy work.

(9) It was his indignity to work under a woman. /It was something he could not bear.

第四节　英语阅读分析与评价活动设计

一、英语阅读分析活动设计

(一)分析的内涵

分析指将材料分解成各组成部分并且确定这些组成部分是如何相互关联的,人们一般将分析看作理解的扩展,或者是评价的前奏。分析包括要素分析、关系分析和组织原理分析,阅读中的分析一般指要素分析和关系分析。

1. 要素分析

所谓要素分析,指能够区分阅读材料的组成要素,表现为能够划分文章的篇章结构,分析主题句、结论句等。这一点与文章结构理解是一样的,这就是为什么有的著作、有些专家把分析作为理解的一部分的原因。

不同体裁的文章构成要素不同,在进行要素分析之前,必须了解各类文章的构成要素。比如故事的构成要素为 who, where, when, why, how 五大要素,而文章的结构可以包括场景、人物、情节、高潮等,文章可能采用倒叙、插叙的方式。说明文和议论文可能采用例证、比较、对照等段落发展模式,其构成要素一般包括论点和论据、主题句、支撑细节、结论句等,要素分析也因此指能够识别、区别这些组成要素。

2. 关系分析

关系包括文章各要素之间的关系、段落之间的关系以及句子之间的关系,单词的指代关系同样属于关系分析的范畴。

文章各要素之间的关系指文章中要素之间的说明与被说明之间的关系,即论点与论据的关系,主题与支撑细节之间的关系,各要素之间的起承转合关系等。

一般来说,段落之间以及句子之间的关系包括递进关系、转折关系、因果关系等。单词的指代关系包括前指和后指,是文章逻辑的纽带,同样是分析的对象。关系的分析同样包括识别论据中的逻辑错误,区分相关陈述与不相关陈述等。

(二)分析类活动的设计

1. 排序

文章的逻辑关系可以表现为逻辑关系的识别和表述,也可以表现为排序、插入等形式。比如,如果学生能将下面的段落正确排序,说明其理解了文章的逻辑。以时间、空间顺序为线索的事物说明文还可以设计

jigsaw reading,将文章里提到的一些细节打乱顺序,然后要求学生根据原文的描写过程,配合常识调整顺序。

例如《大学体验英语》第二册第六单元 *Sports and Health* 是一篇以人为主的记叙文,下例摘选了文中若干连贯的细节,要求根据课文的内容和逻辑顺序重新排序。

Read the following sentences, and re-arrange them according to the essay. Note the conjunctions at the beginning of each sentence.

a. He said that selfless service can make a true hero, and he also hoped that his story would inspire other people.

b. Younger skaters consistently defeated him, yet he kept practicing and competing.

c. Then he finished second in the 1992 Olympics in France and became a hero.

d. While not dazzled by the glory, he remained very modest and did not consider himself a hero.

e. Paul Wiley was a 27-year-old American ice skater who could never win the big competitions.

f. At the same time, fame and endorsements came his way.

g. After his victory in 1992, applause greeted him as he stepped off the plane bringing him home from the Olympics.

h. Many times he considered retirement but he persevered.

2. 插入

所谓插入,指将所给某个段落插入到已有文本中。比如,可以将上面的材料进行改编,把其中一段抽出来让学生将其放到文章中适当的位置。如果学生能够正确插入某段文字,则说明其能够理解文章的逻辑。如果有意安排这种类型的分析活动,最好不采用课本,而是将阅读资料用散页形式发给学生,在PPT上只显示需要插入的部分。这种练习培养的是学生的整体逻辑性。① 在处理记叙文时也可以将倒叙或插叙作为活动的着眼点,例如《大学英语》第三版第三册 *The Day Mother*

---

① 王耿正,曹殿俊,黄付巧. 高中英语阅读教学理论应用研究[M]. 长春:吉林人民出版社,2019.

Cried 第 1—6 段是一个倒叙结构段,可以设计成下面这样的活动:

Assign the task.

The story we are going to read applies flashback writing strategy. Now would you insert the first 6 paragraphs into its proper place according to the time sequence?

Coming home from school that dark winter's day so long ago, I was filled with anticipation. I had a new issue of my favorite sports magazine tucked under my arm, and the house to myself. Dad was at work, my sister was away, and mother wouldn't be home from her new job for an hour. I bounded up the steps, burst into the living room and flipped on a light.

I was shocked into stillness by what I saw. Mother, pulled into a tight ball with her face in her hands, sat at the far end of the couch. She was crying. I had never seen her cry.

I approached cautiously and touched her shoulder. "Mother?" I said. "What's happened?"

She took a long breath and managed a weak smile. "It's nothing, really. Nothing important. Just that I'm going to lose this new job. I can't type fast enough."

"But you've only been there three days,"I said. "You'll catch on." I was repeating a line she had spoken to me a hundred times when I was having trouble learning or doing something important to me.

"No," she said sadly. "I always said I could do anything I set my mind to, and I still think I can in most things. But I can't do this."

练习要求学生根据时间顺序的线索把倒叙部分或插叙部分重新安排位置,使原文全部符合时间顺序。通过关键词的寻找,我们发现这是母亲做打字员时的情况,按照时间顺序应当发生在 17—18 段之间。

3. 问答讨论

回答问题是一个十分灵活的活动形式,同样可以用于分析活动,要求学生分析所给语言材料,回答相关问题。如标点符号在文章中的作用

第三章　英语阅读教学设计概述

就可以通过问答讨论的方式。下面的句子都选自《大学英语》第三版第二册 *My First Job*，我们可以组织学习讨论其中冒号、分号和破折号的作用。

• It proved an awkward journey：a train；a ride and then a walk.

• He proceeded to ask me a number of questions：what subjects I had taken in my General School Certificate；how old I was；what games I played；

• I was dismayed at the thought of teaching algebra and geometry——two subjects at which I had been completely incompetent at school.

• This was the last straw. I was very young；the prospect of working under a woman constituted the ultimate indignity.

说明文最适合设计整体谋篇的分析活动，肢解文章的整体结构，分析各部分之间的逻辑类型，分辨材料和主旨等。当然这种练习还可以让学生熟悉表顺序的连词的功能。例如：

• What aspects did the author mention in the description to fully describe…？

• Where did the author reveal the object he introduced?

• Why did the author announce the name of the object at the end of the description?

4. 要素配对

有些作品直接引语比较多，或者交错表达两种相反的见解，阅读过程会比较混乱。为了构建清晰的逻辑，可以为学生提供图表和相应的要素，让学生进行配对，将文章内容肢解后形成中心紧凑的两个句群。

对比性的说明文有两种写法，或者一段全部写 A 事物的情况，然后再描写 B 事物的情况；或者就某一方面把 A 和 B 进行优劣对比，然后逐条对比。在这种文章中，我们可以设计配对性练习。根据文章的表达，进行配对。如果学生本身水平比较高，还可以变成不完整的表格，让学生根据文章的描述补充不完整的信息。

二、英语阅读评价类活动设计

(一)评价的内涵

1. 什么是评价

评价指为了某种目的,对观念、作品、答案、方法和资料等所做的价值判断,评价包含用准则和标准对这些项目的准确性、有效性、经济性、满意度等进行评估。评价涉及对知识、理解、运用、分析和综合等所有其他行为的某种组合,认知要求、语言能力要求都相当高,大学阶段的英语教学要求学生达到评价的认知目标。

2. 评价的种类

根据评价标准的不同,评价可以分为内部标准参照评价和外部标准参照评价。

(1)内部标准参照评价

内部标准参照评价来自阅读材料自身,指根据所阅读文章推断出来的逻辑、结构、论点等,然后根据文章呈现的结构要求、逻辑关系、观点论点,判断所给语篇是否与所阅读文章结构一致、逻辑关系相符,根据文中的观点判断所给陈述是否正确。如求职信的结构,根据每部分包含的内容等,判断所给求职信是否符合要求。

(2)外部标准参照评价

外部标准参照评价来自阅读材料之外,其内容较为广泛,可以指评价者自身的标准,可以指评价者所处的社会环境中通用的标准。就阅读而言,一般情况下"What do you think of the author?""What do you think of his argument?""What would you do if you were…?"等属于利用评价者自身的标准进行评价。因为每个人的评价标准不同,对作者的评价以及对其观点的评价也就不同,所选择的行为方式也不同,这种设计有利于同学之间的讨论和协商。而"Do you think they will happen in China?""Will these things happen in your universities?""Will Chinese students accept such offer?"则要求学生根据通用的标准评价而不是自己的标准评价。学生需要考虑在中国环境下人们的价值标准,中国高校是否允许某类事情发生,中国的学生能否接受某种恩惠等等。此时,评价者所依据的是外部标准,由于这种评价不会太受个人情感态度的左右,同学们的看法应该大体一致,因此有利于小组讨论活动的设计。

(二)评价活动的设计原则

1. 支架原则

支架原则指的是在设计评价活动时要考虑支架的搭建。要实施有效合理的评价首先必须明确评价的标准,如果是内部标准参照评价,教师就应该设计标准认识活动,分析所阅读的材料中包含的逻辑、结构等,然后提供要评价的材料。

2. 评价分享原则

由于人们价值观的差异,所做的价值判断也会不同。在实施外部标准参照评价,尤其是依据学生个人标准进行评价时,教师可以充分利用学生评价方式与评价结论上可能存在的差异组织学生开展小组讨论,分享观点,促进理解。

以《大学英语精读》第三版第二册第一单元 At the Dinner Party 为例,文章讲述了晚宴期间,女主人在眼镜蛇爬过她的脚面时,为了不打草惊蛇以免伤害到其他的客人而表现出的勇敢和冷静。教师可根据该故事设计一个评价活动,要求学生来评价女主人当时的表现,或者要求学生换位思考,如果自己是这位女主人,自己当时又会怎么做?

What do you think of the hostess?

Step 1 Assign the learning task.

Directions: What do you think of the hostess in the story? Do you think she is so brave? Why or why not? If you were her, what would you do at that time?

Step 2 Students share their ideas within groups of four.

Step 3 Students report about group ideas.

针对这样的评价活动,学生可能会存在不同的理解和对女主人行为的评价。那么教师可指导学生在小组内部进行讨论,相互阐述自己的观点,分享对女主人行为的理解和评价。另外,教师可组织学生进行评价汇报,每组选出代表在全班同学面前展示自己的讨论结果。其他学生则可以作为听众来评价演讲同学的评价。这样不仅可以加深学生对文章的理解,还可以分享学生不同的评价,相互理解、相互促进、相互提高。

3. 理解原则

所谓理解原则,指评价以促进学生对课文的理解为目标,通过评价学生可以更好地理解文章的结构、逻辑和语言使用,可以更好地理解文章所要传达的观点、理念、价值观。如果只是为评价而评价,评价也就失去了应有的作用。

以《大学英语精读》第三版第三册第五单元 The Day Mother Cried 为例。在本文作者的眼里,母亲一直以来都是很坚强的。所以当作者第一次看到母亲哭泣时,惊讶之外也多了份自责,因为自己从来没有体会过母亲的压力。不过,母亲并没有畏惧,最终战胜了困难,这也成了作者日后成功的动力。该故事比较贴近生活,反映的主题思想也比较容易被学生接受和理解。教师可以根据该故事设计一个评价活动,让学生评价本文中母亲的哭泣行为,或者换位思考,如何看待自己父母的哭泣行为。

• Activity 1 What do you think of the mother?

Step 1 Assign the learning task.

This story describes a mother who was found crying before her child for the first time, which makes the author surprised and embarrassed. What do you think of the mother in the story? Do you think she is a weak person by crying before her child? Why or why not? If you were her, would you do the same?

Step 2 Students share their ideas within groups of four.

Step 3 Students report about group ideas.

• Activity 2 Similar cases.

Step 1 Assign the learning task.

Have you ever seen your mother or father crying? If so, what do you think of them? Do you think they are weak by doing that?

Step 2 Students discuss in pairs.
Step 3 Call on students to share their ideas.

此类评价活动虽然属于口头活动,对学生的口语表达能力有一定的要求,但还是应该以理解为主。因此,通过这样的评价活动,学生不仅可以加深对文章中那位母亲的理解,而且还可以通过类似情况换位思考,加深对自己父母的认识和理解。这样的评价活动目标不是训练学生的语言表达能力,更不是为了评价的形式,而是更好地理解文章所表达的主旨大意和中心思想,更好地提升学生的认知水平和理解能力。

第四章　英语阅读教学之学习策略探索

在英语阅读教学过程中,英语教师需要科学、合理地设计阅读教学活动,帮助学生快速进入学习状态。学生想要提升自身的英语阅读能力,不仅需要合理配合老师的教学活动,还需要掌握一定的阅读策略。为此,本章针对英语阅读教学之学习策略展开分析。

第一节　英语阅读策略分析

一、学习策略

(一)学习策略的定义

学习策略是指人们在学习过程中使用的技巧和方法。学习不同的学科,比如外语、数学、物理、化学、生物、地理等,所使用的技巧和方法也不同,这些技巧和方法就称为各个学科的学习策略。

外语学习策略是指在外语学习过程中学习者所采用的学习技巧或方法,是摸索单词、语法规则和其他语言项目的含义和用法的方法。使用学习策略可以提高学习效率。

外语学习策略在国外称为 language learning strategies,即"语言学习策略"或简称"学习策略"。这是因为学习不同的语言——不论是学习母语还是外语——使用的策略均相似。

(二)学习策略的分类

学习策略有多种分类方法,下面介绍在国外广为人们所接受的一种分类方法。

(1)认知策略(cognitive strategies),如根据上下文猜测词义的策略。

(2)交际策略(communication strategies),如为了交际需要弥补词汇量的不足,用 an underwater ship (水下的船)代替 submarine(潜水艇)。

(3)社交情感策略(social affective strategies),如在学习中遇到困难与别人讨论,或争取更多的机会与母语为英语的本族人交流。

以上三种策略均有助于外语学习。根据著名语言学家 Kubin 的观点,认知策略所起的作用是直接的,而另外两种策略则是间接的。

从外语学习的角度,还可将学习策略分为词汇学习策略、阅读策略、会话策略和写作策略。① 会话策略是指上面提到的"交际策略"。而词汇、阅读和写作策略,总的来说,可以归为上面所述的"认知策略",如记忆单词的策略、阅读过程中的归纳推理方法以及写作中谋篇布局的技巧等。

二、阅读策略

在阅读过程中,借助上下文、文章结构以及背景知识等线索理解词语、段落或全文的意思称为阅读策略,比如借助上下文线索推测词义或根据篇章结构线索迅速捕捉文章大意。

根据上下文等线索可以将阅读策略分为六大类,如表 4-1 所示。

---

① 刘津开. 大学英语阅读策略训练[M]. 广州:华南理工大学出版社,2006.

表 4-1　英语阅读策略分类

类	次类	次次类
1. 逻辑关系线索	1A 因果 1B 转折、对照、让步 1C 排比并列 1D 指代关系 1E 语篇衔接	
	1F 词语搭配	1Fa 动词＋名词 1Fb 形容词(或名词)＋名词 1Fc 名词＋动词 1Fd 动词＋副词
2. 信息查询线索(查询)	2A 大写字母 2B 阿拉伯数字 2C 目录、标题、索引 2D 栏目、图片 2E 搜索引擎	
3. 捕捉大意线索(浏览)	3A 捕捉文章大意线索 3B 捕捉段落大意线索 3C 捕捉一本书的大意线索	
4. 背景知识线索	4A 经历、情景、常识 4B 语法知识	
	4C 词形线索	4Ca 前缀、后缀、词根 4Cb 大小写 4Cc 缩写 4Cd 读音 4Ce 字形

续表

类	次类	次次类
5. 篇章结构线索	5A 记叙文文体结构	5Aa 新闻报道文体结构
	5B 描写文文体结构	
	5C 说明文文体结构	5Ca 主题句线索
	5D 议论文文体结构	5 Da
6. 释义线索	6A 定义 6B 示例 6C 重述	

(一)逻辑关系线索

逻辑关系线索是指文章上下文中的单词、短语、句子和段落相互之间存在的逻辑关系,如因果,转折、对照、让步,排比、并列关系等。借助逻辑关系线索进行阅读是一种主要的阅读策略,有助于阅读理解。例如,在"The child is always on the periphery, never in the center."句中,never 表意转折,由此推测 periphery 与 center 意思相反。

(二)信息查询线索

信息查询线索是指文章上下文提供的有助于快速查找有关信息的各种线索,比如大写字母、阿拉伯数字、目录、标题、索引。借助上下文线索以及网上搜索引擎快速查询信息是生活中最常使用的阅读策略之一。

(三)捕捉大意线索

捕捉大意线索主要指有关文体修辞和篇章结构方面的特点。依据文体修辞和篇章结构的特点迅速捕捉文章或段落的大意也是一种常用的阅读策略。

(四)篇章结构线索

篇章结构是指文章的文体结构。文章可以按照不同的文体归类为说明文、议论文、记叙文、应用文等。不同文体的文章,其篇章结构不同。了解各类文章的文体结构特点有助于提高阅读的速度、理解能力和效果。①

(五)释义线索

释义线索是指在文章或句子中作者所提供的对生词的解释,如定义、示例或重述。通常这种解释比较通俗易懂,与词典中的释义相同或相近。但有时作者对某词语的释义与词典的意思不尽相同,因此借助释义线索可以增进理解,提高阅读速度。

第二节 英语阅读策略之逻辑关系

逻辑关系线索是指文章或句子中的生词与其上下文中的其他词语的逻辑关系,如因果、转折、对照、让步、排比、并列关系等。借助逻辑关系线索推测词语的意思是常用的一种阅读策略。下面举例说明几种常见的逻辑关系线索,然后概述在英语阅读过程中如何利用逻辑关系线索提高阅读理解能力。

---

① 孟留军. 大学英语阅读实训[M]. 合肥:安徽大学出版社,2018.

第四章　英语阅读教学之学习策略探索

一、逻辑关系线索分类与示例

(一)因果关系

文章上下文中的某些词语与生词之间的因果关系,包括假定的条件与预测在此条件下所产生的结果之间的因果关系,如 if 条件从句与主句之间的关系。

The football match had to be canceled on account of the awful weather.(由于恶劣的天气,足球赛只得 canceled。)

本句主要线索是 on account of(由于),在上下文中不难猜出 canceled 的词义为"取消"。

A new farming technique having been worked out, the yields as a whole increased by 20 percent.(由于一种新的耕种技术已研制出来,总的 yields 提高了 20%。)

本句逗号前部分是分词的独立主格结构,可以表示原因、伴随状态等。即使不了解这部分的语法结构,也不难推断出该句前后两部分含有因果关系。据此可以猜出 yields 的意思为"收成,产量"。

The manager lost his temper just because his secretary was ten minutes late.(经理只是因为他的秘书迟到了 10 分钟就 lost his temper。)

根据句中的 because 和上下文线索不难猜出 lost his temper 的意思是"发怒,生气"。

His story about being attacked on the way home was hardly credible, he didn't have a mark on him.(他所讲述的在回家的路上遭受攻击几乎不 credible,他身上一点伤痕都没有。)

虽然该句中没有表示因果关系的连接词,可是逗号前后部分的因果关系显而易见,由此不难推测 credible 的意思为"令人相信的,可信的"。

His business would be lucrative if he followed his father's advice.(如果听从他父亲的忠告,他的生意会 lucrative。)

根据上下文和常识不难猜出 lucrative 的意思是"赚钱的"。

(二)转折、对照、让步关系

文章上下文中的某些词语与生词之间的转折、对照或让步关系。

Most of us dream of being immortal, but in reality no one would like to live forever.(我们很多人都渴望immortal,但是实际上没有人愿意永久地活下去。)

本句主要线索是 but,表示转折,由此可推断 immortal 与 not live forever 的意思相反,即"永生,长生不死"。

They had come saying that they would ameliorate the problems in that place, however, they had only succeeded in making them worse. (他们来时说要 ameliorate 那一地区的问题,可是他们的所作所为只是使问题变得更糟。)

本句主要线索是 however,表示转折,因此可推断 ameliorate 与 make…worse 的意思应相反,即 make…better "使变好;改善"。

The child is always on the periphery, never in the center; the wishes of the parents come first. (孩子从来都不是位于中心,而总是处在 periphery;父母的意愿是第一位的。)

本句中的主要线索是 never,表示转折,由此可推断 periphery 与 center 的意思相反,在上下文中的意思应是"边上,外围,次要的位置"。

Notwithstanding his inexperience, the new minister has already won respect for his energy and honesty. (Notwithstanding 新部长没经验,他的充沛的精力和正直已经赢得了人们的尊敬。)

根据本句大意,可以判断前后分句含有让步关系,由此可推测该词的意思为"尽管"。

They carried on in spite of the extremely difficult conditions. (尽管条件极为困难,他们还是 carried on。)

根据 in spite of(尽管)线索,不难猜出 carried on 的意思为"坚持下去,继续干"。

(三)指代关系

通俗地讲,指代关系是指一个代词(如 he、she、they、this、these 等)

与它所指的某个词或词语之间的关系,比如在"Tom is a student. He goes to school every day."句中,代词 He 与 Tom 之间的关系。这种关系显而易见,因此对英语学习者来说并不难理解掌握。然而,在阅读过程中,尤其遇到较难理解的句子、段落或有生词的语句时,这种指代关系往往被忽略。现举一例说明。

读下面一段短文,猜一猜词 proponents 的意思。

People who want more economic growth, on the other hand, argue that even at the present growth rate there are still many poor people in the world. These proponents of economic growth believe that only more growth can create the capital needed to improve the quality of life in the world. Furthermore, they argue that only continued growth can provide the financial resources required to protect our natural surroundings from industrialization.

其实借助指代关系线索不难猜。在第 2 句中的代词 these 将该句与上一句连接起来。proponents 指上句中的复数名词,或指句首的 people,或指句尾的 poor people。究竟指哪一个 people,应依据主要线索 on the other hand。此线索意为"在另一方面",其作用是将本段与上一段连接起来。上一段讲述反对者的意见,他们认为经济增长过快会导致许多问题。本段中的 on the other hand 表示相反,介绍赞同经济增长的人的观点。由此不难猜出 proponents 的意思是"支持者"。

(四)语篇衔接

在一篇文章中,尤其是说明文或论说文中,句与句之间、段与段之间通常用词或短语将意思连接起来。了解文章中使用的衔接手段有助于提高我们的阅读理解能力,读懂难句,使我们读得更快、更轻松。语篇衔接手段可分为两种:句与句衔接、段与段衔接。现举一例说明。

When writing an application, one should bear in mind that the readers will know little about China. So you should supply details that establish why a given fact in your record is significant.

Likewise, recently I was looking at an application from a student who ranked fifth in his province on the national university entrance exam. The province, as it happens, has some 35 million inhabitants, …

以上例子选自一篇文章两段的开头，文章主题是留学美国如何填写申请材料，如何写个人简历。了解第2段主题或中心思想的主要线索是段首的连接词"likewise"，其作用是承上启下，与上一段连接起来。上一段第1句是主题句：When writing an application, one should bear in mind that the readers will know little about China.（填申请表时应注意读者对中国了解甚少）。第1段中其他句子是举例说明此主题。通过衔接词 Likewise 获悉第1、2段的主题相同，第2段举例进一步说明该主题。借助衔接手段（比如 Likewise）有助于我们了解文章的篇章结构，比如在上例两段中，第1段第1句是主题句，其余部分是举例说明。篇章结构有助于我们快速了解文章或段落的大意，尤其对阅读生词较多的文章时更是如此。

二、如何利用逻辑关系线索提高阅读理解能力

首先，在阅读中注意句与句、段与段之间的逻辑关系，学会识别文章中的各种逻辑关系。逻辑关系有两种：一种是明示的，可以借助某些标志性的词语识别出来，比如某些连接词语 but, however, on the contrast 表示转折对照关系，because, due to 表示因果关系等；另一种逻辑关系是隐含的，即句与句、段与段之间虽然没有标志性的连接词语但隐含某种逻辑关系。

识别隐含的逻辑关系可以依据：①语法知识，比如独立主格结构、介词短语、分词短语等用于表示原因、伴随状态等；②标点符号；③文体修辞知识。[1]

学会识别文章中的各种逻辑关系靠日积月累。在平时学习英语时，如听课、听录音、阅读、做练习，应特别留意文章中出现的连接词语，如表示"一……就"的意思可以用下列词语引起状语从句：as soon as, no sooner…than, hardly…when, scarcely…when, immediately, the moment, the minute 等。比如表示因果关系、假设因果关系的连接词语有：because, as, since, for, now that, seeing that 等。这些连接词语如同人体的关节、机器的连接点或房屋的框架结构，用心记住它们，对于英语阅读理解、英

---

[1] 王婷婷,刘硕,魏纪福.英语阅读与教学研究[M].广州:广东旅游出版社,2018.

语学习有事半功倍之效。

仅学会识别文章中的各种逻辑关系还不够,提高阅读能力还要靠大量实践。道理很简单,语言学习如同练打字、学游泳,从某种意义上说,是一种技能训练。知道键盘的指法但练得少就不可能打得快,知道蛙泳的姿势动作要领但未经足够的训练也不可能学会游泳。英语阅读亦然,仅了解有哪些阅读策略是不够的,还需要靠大量的阅读实践。

总之,在英语阅读过程中应特别注意思考,读与思密不可分。阅读理解是一种思维过程,是综合分析、归纳、推理的过程。在这一过程中,思维不是主观臆断的,而是客观的,即依据文章中提供的种种线索,借助我们的常识、背景知识、文体知识、语法知识等去分析判断综合。由此不难看出,阅读理解过程不是被动的,而是主动的。以上讨论逻辑关系线索旨在帮助英语学习者学会主动地阅读,边读边思考,从而达到读得又快又好的目的。

第三节　英语阅读策略之略读

一、浏览

浏览是指通过快速阅读或跳读了解一篇文章或某一段落的大意。浏览大意是我们生活中最常用的阅读技能之一。在学习、工作中经常需要阅读一些资料,如学习参考书、文件等。这种阅读是有选择的,即读相关的书、文章或资料。比如,找到一本参考书或文章后,首先要浏览一下,迅速了解它的大概内容,然后决定是否需要将它作为参考资料进一步细读。

浏览不是逐字逐句读,而是需要一些技巧方法。下面谈一谈如何浏览以便快速捕捉一篇文章、一个段落或一本书的大意。

(一)如何快速捕捉文章大意

1. 篇名和大小标题

阅读一篇文章的题目以及文章各节中的大小标题可以使读者粗略了解文章的大意。

2. 每段段首

如果想更准确或更详尽地了解文章大意,可以阅读每段段首,并根据文体知识判断文章属于哪种文体:记叙文、描写文、说明文和议论文等。

3. 根据不同文体采取不同的浏览方法

(1)记叙文

捕捉文章大意应抓住5个"Wh"(When,Where,Who,What,Why),即在何时、何地、何人发生了何事、是何原因。浏览时,只读与这五点相关的信息,而不相干的信息可忽略不读。

新闻报道属记叙文文体。通常阅读新闻报道的第一段即可了解新闻内容大意。

(2)说明文或议论文

阅读首尾段即可捕捉文章大意。如果理解有困难或想更详尽地了解文章大意,可以阅读每段段首,因为此类文体的文章每段段首通常点明该段的主题或中心思想。

(二)如何快速捕捉段落大意

(1)首先要快速了解文章大意,具体方法见上述内容。

(2)如上所述,阅读每段段首,粗略了解文章的大意。

(3)如果理解本段有困难,应阅读上一段,捕捉其中心思想。尤其注意读上一段的结尾,因为上段末尾与本段段首衔接。

(4)如果采取以上三个步骤理解本段大意还有困难,则要对文章的篇章结构进行分析。比如,文章属说明文或议论文,那么先读第一段,找出该段的主题句。首段主题通常也是文章讨论的主题,然后阅读各段段首,确定文章从几个方面讨论其主题。掌握文章的总体框架之后,就可得知本段属于此框架的哪一部分。① 至此,再重复以上三个步骤即可理解本段大意。

(三)如何快速捕捉一本书的大意

(1)阅读书名和内容提要。
(2)阅读书中的序言和目录。
(3)浏览第一章。第一章通常是绪论,一般在该章的结尾要简要介绍其他各章的内容。
(4)如果要更详细地了解书中内容,可以快速浏览各章内容。

二、查询

(一)上网查询

1. 利用搜索引擎

利用 Internet 查询资料简单、快速而方便。查找资料要使用搜索引擎。常用的搜索引擎有:百度,Google 等。

2. 如何输入关键词

(1)输入英文关键词查英文资料

在网上查询英文资料简单、方便。搜索引擎"Google"和"Yahoo"通常适于英文资料查询。但对于普通人来说,最简单方便的搜索工具是"飓风"。比如想查一下美国 NBA 大球星乔丹是哪一年出生的,可以按以下步骤查询:

输入关键词。输入英文单词:"Jordan NBA birthday"。注意单词

---

① 刘津开. 大学英语阅读策略训练[M]. 广州:华南理工大学出版社,2006.

间要有空格。

　　查看搜索结果。在"飓风"屏幕上分别点击查看 10 个搜索引擎的搜索结果。查看结果发现只有"V21CN"（21 世纪搜索引擎）的搜索结果显示了相关信息：

　　Feet　Socks：NBA Medium Low；Shoes：Any Jordans Information First Name：Michael；Last Name：Jordan；Birth Year：1963；Birth Month：February；Birthday：17；Birth City：Brooklyn…

　　结果显示乔丹是 1963 年出生的。

　　分析搜索结果。首先要判断以上搜索结果是否可靠真实。有两点质疑：一是此资料源于电脑游戏，二是 Jordan 会不会是同名同姓而不是同一个人。

　　"飓风"中的其他 9 个引擎的搜索结果，除了"V3721"引擎显示了一些 Jordan 的信息（但没有出生年份），其余引擎都搜索失败。

　　从"V21CN"的搜索结果中得知乔丹的全名是 Michael Jordan，由此可得知 8 个引擎搜索失败的原因。Jordan 是姓，Michael 是名。输入关键词 Jordan，如同输入中文的姓氏"张、王、李、赵"，根本无法查询。

　　输入不同的关键词核对搜索结果。输入英文单词：Michael Jordan NBA birth，注意使用 Google 和 Yahoo 搜索引擎核对比较可靠，因为它们是很大的英文网站。Google 的搜索结果，如下所示，证实第一次搜索结果真实可靠。

　　Michael Jordan biography bio-［翻译此页 BETA］

　　Michael Jeffrey Jordan was born on February 17, 1963, in Brooklyn, New York, but his family decided to move to… The team had such college players as Jordan, Patrick Ewing, Chris Mullin(NBA players weren't allowed to compete in the…

　　(2)输入中文关键词查中文资料

　　步骤同上（输入英文关键词查英文资料）。

　　(3)输入英文关键词查中文资料

　　想要知道一英文词语，比如 Gone with the Wind 的中文意思，可以使用"飓风"搜索，步骤如下：

　　输入中英文关键词"Gone with the Wind 风"。注意一定要输入一个与英文词相关的汉字或词组，否则查询结果仅显示英文。

　　查看搜索结果。虽然有搜索结果，但无法断定该词语的中文意思。

重新输入英文关键词,更换中文关键词。如果我们知道该词语是电影名,可输入"Gone with the Wind 电影"。如果知道该词语是小说名,可输入"Gone with the Wind 小说",然后使用"飓风"搜索。

查看搜索结果。上一段讲的两种关键词输入法都可以搜索到该词语的中文意思:《飘》或《乱世佳人》两种译法。

核对搜索结果。如果不能确定搜查结果是否可靠,应更换关键词重新输入搜寻,步骤同上文(输入英文关键词查英文资料)。

(4)输入中文关键词查英文资料

输入中文关键词查英文资料的步骤同上述的(3)差不多。比如想知道"三国演义"怎样用英文表达,可用"飓风"查询。输入关键词"三国演义 three",注意必须输入一个相关的英文单词,否则搜索结果只有中文,而没有英文。搜索结果显示三种译法,从中选择自己认为最适当的译法:The Romance of Three Kingdoms。

上网查询资料既快又方便,利用搜索引擎查询的步骤不难掌握,在上面已举例说明。比较难处理的问题是搜索结果往往出现多个结果,需要从中选择一个。

(二)利用校园网内部资源查询

一般高校图书馆都有大量的电子资源,电子资源包括"中国学术会议全文数据库"和其他各种数据库,仅国内外学术期刊就有上万种。电子资源都有简单便利的检索系统,利用这种资源学习研究,方便、省时、效率高。

第四节 英语阅读策略之篇章结构

篇章结构指文章的文体结构。文章可以按照不同的文体归类为说明文、记叙文、应用文等。说明文是一种介绍或说明性的文体。记叙文指故事、小说等。应用文包括广告、请帖、通知、留言、借条、收条、请假条等。不同文体的文章,其篇章结构不同。了解各类文章的文体结构特点有助于提高我们阅读的速度、理解能力和效果。

一、文体结构概述

下面简要介绍四种主要文体结构。

(一)记叙文

1. 记叙文的含义

我们把记叙人物的经历或实践的发生、发展和变化过程的文章叫做记事文或叙述文,记叙文通常包含以下要素:时间(when),地点(where),人物(who),事件(what),原因(why),结果(how)。其中时间、地点、人物最为重要,广义上说,记叙文包括按照一定的逻辑或者时间顺序叙述的真实或者虚构的历史、自传、故事、新闻等,记叙文以记人叙事为主要内容。

2. 记叙文的特点

记叙文有着显著的特点,主要表现在以下三个方面:事件特殊、情节合理、语言生动形象。

(1)事件特殊

记叙文的范围十分广泛,所叙说的事件可以是惊天动地的大事,也可以是刻骨铭心的小事,但不管是大事还是小事,事件本身对于作者甚至是当事人、读者来说都具有一定特殊的意义,都是值得回忆或令人感动的事情。

(2)情节合理

一篇好的文章,通常具有跌宕起伏的合理的情节、清晰的线索,读者会跟着写作者的节奏,对主人公的言行举止以及事情的进一步发展结局产生浓厚的兴趣,最后还在脑海中形成深刻的印象。能达到这种效果的文章一定是具备了情节合理的重要特点。

(3)语言生动形象

语言生动形象是记叙文最显著的特点。因为记叙文要描写特殊的事件、曲折的情节,必须依托生动形象的语言。在这里,语言的生动形象并非指优美的语言、华丽的辞藻、夸张的表达,而是指具体、贴近生活,使人倍感亲切的语言。其实,用朴实无华的语言将发生的事情真切地表达出来,使读者身临其境,并非易事,这离不开作者深刻的文字功底和切身的生活体会。

(二)描写文

1. 描写文的含义

描写文是用生动形象的语言、精细入微的语言描绘人物的状态、动作、景物的性质、特征的一种文体。描写文的主要特点主要在造型性和实感性上,主要目的是用唯美的语言描绘栩栩如生的形象,让读者读后留下深刻的印象,描写与叙述密切相连,在文章中二者尝尝穿插运用。

2. 描写的方法

描写的对象不同,描写的方法就不同。根据描写的对象可以将描写分为人物描写、场景描写、地点描写、物体描写。下面就针对描写对象来介绍描写的方法。

(1)人物描写

在进行人物描写时,首先要抓住人物的外貌、语言、行为及心理特征,这样文章才会写得生动而饱满。

外貌描写。对于人物的外貌的描写,除了展示出人物的精神世界和个性气质之外,还要显示出主题人物的身份、爱好、职业、经历以及遭遇。外貌描写顾名思义就是对人物的外貌特征进行描写,以达到揭示人物的思想性格,表达作者的喜爱与厌恶,加深读者对人物的印象。

语言描写。语言描写即描写人物的言谈话语,包括对话、独白等。透过语言,往往可以窥见一个人的思想和性格。

行动描写。行动描写是通过语言文字表现人物自身在矛盾斗争中的行动,来展示人物的性格特征和精神面貌的描写。行动描写是反映人物思想、性格、心理等的有效手段之一。

心理描写。心理描写,就是以语言文字对人物的内心世界、性格特征、道德品质所进行的描写。因为一个人的心理活动可以反映出一个人的内心世界,所以,在进行心理描写时应注意:应写指定的人物在特定的事件或者环境下必然产生的内心的活动,不能单纯地为心理描写去进行心理描写;要最大限度地写清楚心理变化过程的细节;心理描写的跌宕起伏要跟故事的情节、人物的动作和表情相辅相成。

(2)场景描写

场景描写是指,作者在生活和自然环境中提取一个有意义的场景,并充分调动各种感官多方位多角度地去观察与体验,然后采用生动简洁的语言、丰富多彩的修辞手法,将看到的、听到的、想到的按照一定的顺序描写下来,给读者以身临其境的感觉。场景描写的首要一点,也是重要的一点,就是观察,只有会用眼观察,才能捕捉住场景特点,才能发现场景中最动人心的一幕,才能有话可写。

(3)地点描写

我们把用生动形象的语言对地点或者环境进行具体逼真描绘的写法叫作地点描写,使读者如临其境,地点环境描写在任何作品中都不可或缺,毕竟人物以及事件的展开都无法脱离社会和自然环境。

地点描写的第一种方法是从整体印象到细节描述,这种方法的特点是突出了文章的主题,进而吸引读者,写法如下:先确定要描写的地点,然后概括第一印象,最后再具体描述。第二种方法是从细节描述到整体印象,这个写法的特点是循序渐进,从具体到一般来启动读者的思维。具体写法是先细心观察要描述的地点,然后逐一列出突出的细节,最后总结整体印象。地点描写与文章中人物的思想和情感有着紧密的关系。

(4)物体描写

物体描写就是对各种动物、植物和各种无生命物体的描写。物体描写也称"状物"。状物是对物体的描摹,类似绘画中的"写生"。状物的目的在于使读者对所描摹的物体有一个准确而鲜明的具体印象;通过对物体的临摹,揭示物体所表达的精神境界和主题思想;以借物抒情的手法,引发自己的情感和思想,点出文章的主题。

3. 描写的手段

(1)白描

我们把不加任何修饰成分、用普通简洁的语言反映事物特质的描写方法称为白描,白描文字直来直去,着墨不多且不带任何渲染色彩,却能穷形尽相,带来与众不同的描写效果。

(2)肖像描写

生动准确的语言描写人们包括身材、服饰、容貌、表情、姿态等外形上的特征即为肖像描写。人的生活经历、喜怒哀乐常常通过表情显露出来,所以肖像描写对刻画人物的形象十分有利。

(3)烘托描写

我们在写作时会碰到一种抽象的事物,这种事物很难通过直接描写来表现,这就需要通过对彼事物的描写达到表现此事物的目的,这就叫做烘托描写。烘托描写可以将抽象的事物幻化成具体的事物,所以对抽象事物的描写也更适合用烘托描写法。

(4)设喻描写

运用比喻等修辞手段的描写方法称为设喻描写。设喻描写常用于写景、状物、描摹事态,而且可以使被描写的事物更加明朗、生动、形象,使被描写的事物更具感染力,使人产生身临其境的感觉。

(三)说明文

说明文是对事物的发生、发展、结果、特征、性质、状态、功能等进行解释、介绍、阐述的一种文体。它是最基本、最常见的一种文体。不同于记叙文那样告人以事,也不同于描写文那样动人以形,说明文旨在通过如实的解说来启发读者,向读者提供知识或给予指导。换言之,说明文的目的是喻人,通过对人或事物的说明、介绍,使读者了解情况、学习知识。内容提要、科普小品或信息量大、知识性强的文章等都在说明文之列。[①]

(四)议论文

1. 议论文的含义

议论文就是作者为表明自己的立场、观点和方法就某个问题、某个

[①] 文亚光,郑春红. 语篇视角下的高中英语阅读教学[M]. 成都:西南交通大学出版社,2019.

现象发表自己的见地和思想，进行深刻的分析和评论的写作方式，目的是"说服"阅读者，即针对某一有争议的问题，为了使读者接受自己的观点和建议，通过摆事实、讲道理来达成共识。我们常见的报纸杂志上的社论和评论文章、决议、宣言、公报以及讨论会上的发言等都属于议论文的范畴。议论文与说明文有时候难以区分，虽然他们关系密切，但是目的是不同的：议论文的目的是劝说读者同意并接受作者的观点，而说明文的目的是客观地解释观念、事物、原则等。

2. 议论文的构成要素

议论文一般包含三个构成要素，分别是论点、论据和论证。在学习英语议论文写作初期，教师要指导学生处理好这三个要素以及它们之间的关系。了解这三者之间的关系是写议论文的关键。

(1) 论点

论点是一篇文章的灵魂，它是作者论述问题的根据，是作者对论述问题提出见解和主张并加以阐释和说明的基本观点。在写作上没有限制论点提出的位置，可以开门见山地提出自己的观点，表明立场，也可以在论述过程中提出，还可以作为结束语提出。需要注意的是，在论述过程中必须做到论点鲜明、严谨、准确，而且论点只能有一个，然后围绕这一论点展开论述。

(2) 论据

有论点必然要有支持和证明论点的论据。所谓论据，就是作者建立观点的依据和议论的基础。论据可以是事实论据也可以是理论论据。无论是哪种论据，在选择的时候要注意以下几点。

论据要真实。所选择的论据首先要真实，否则文章就会失去说服力。

论据要与论点紧密相连。所选择的论据一定要紧紧围绕论点展开，而且还要与最终的结论相吻合。

论据要充分。要阐述一个论点，必须选取足够多的论据，如果论据过少，则不足以说明论点。

论据要典型。所选择的论据要最能反映事物的本质，而典型的事例最能体现事物的本质，所以要选择典型的事例。

(3) 论证

论证，是议论文的第三大要素。作者运用论据来证明论点的过程和方法就是论证，表明了论据和论点的逻辑关系，论证是说服读者接受论点的关键，要使论证组织得强硬有力就要准确阐明论点和论据、观点和事实之间的逻辑关系，这样文章结构才能统一、严谨、完整。

3. 议论文的组成形式

议论文的组成形式有很多种，最为常见的是"三段式"。所谓三段式，就是作者按照引言段、主体段和结尾段三个部分进行写作，表达文章主题。

(1)引言段

引言段由引言句、背景介绍和主旨句三要素组成，引言段的作用就是引出全文的段落，用引言句介绍作者要论述的话题，背景介绍表明与主题相关的背景，主旨句的作用是点明文章的发展方向。

(2)主体段

主体段是文章论据的集中部分，也是文章的核心部分。主体段可以是一整个大段落，也可以分为几个小段，每一个段落都有一个主题句，每一个主题句都是主旨句的有力说明与论证。需要注意的是，在写主体段时，所选用的论据必须准确、真实、充分，并紧密联系论点，这样才能将问题表达清楚。

(3)结尾段

文章提出观点并论证了观点之后，要进行文章的结尾段的写作，目的在于重申整个文章的主题加以恰当的评论，给读者一个顺其自然的结尾，让读者对文章的观点深信不疑，一个好的结尾段会给读者带来一个完整的阅读体验。结尾段有两种写法：一种是总结正文，另一种是转换手法重述文章的命题。

二、如何使用篇章结构线索

了解文章的篇章结构特点有助于提高阅读效率。下面谈一谈怎样利用篇章结构线索阅读。首先讨论记叙文，然后谈说明文和议论文。这三种文体是日常生活中最常见的文体，也是大学生接触最多的文体。与这三种文体相比，描写文使用的频率就低得多，描写多穿插于事件的记叙中或说明文和议论文中。

(一)根据记叙文的篇章结构线索快速捕捉文章大意

了解文章的篇章结构特点有助于阅读理解,快速捕捉文章大意。下面举例说明。阅读下面短文,了解文章大意。

Trio Sentenced for Counterfeit Note Offences

Three men, aged between 32 and 40, were sentenced to five to eight years imprisonment at the Court of First Instance today (June 2) for counterfeit note offences.

The court heard that after extensive investigations, officers of Police Commercial Crime Bureau raided a residential unit in Yuen Long on 9 January, 2004.

The trio were arrested after 3,450 pieces of finished and semi-finished counterfeit HK $500 banknotes and a large quantity of counterfeiting paraphernalia was seized in the premises.

Investigations revealed that the counterfeit banknotes were directly produced by two ink-jet printers and they could be distinguished when compared with genuine banknotes.

Among the arrested persons, a 40-year-old man was charged with counterfeiting banknotes with intent, custody of counterfeit banknotes with intent, custody of counterfeiting implements with intent and possession of a dangerous drug. The other two men, both aged 32, were charged with counterfeiting banknotes with intent and custody of counterfeit banknotes with intent.

The trio were found guilty at the Court of First Instance on May 6, 2005 and the sentence was meted out today.

The 40-year-old man and one of the 32-year-old men pleaded guilty to their charges and were sentenced to six years, and five years' imprisonment respectively. Another 32-year-old man pleaded not guilty and was sentenced to eight years' imprisonment.

浏览上面的短文,马上会发现这是一篇新闻报道。读新闻报道时,一般仅读第1段就可以迅速了解文章大意。从第1段会得知When, Where, What,即何时、何地、发生了什么:6月2日在法庭有3个人因制

第四章 英语阅读教学之学习策略探索

贩假币分别被判刑 5—8 年。

新闻报道属记叙文,其篇章结构的特点是首段概述主要内容,其他部分对发生的事件详细描述。获悉文章大意后再读细节,可以读得更快,理解得更透彻。

更重要的是,了解文章大意后再读,能够抓住要点,忽略不相关的细节,因此提高阅读效率。在日常生活中,阅读是为了摄取信息。比如读报,一份报纸通常有几十页,周末上百页。细读每项内容不可能,没有那么多的时间。一般我们先浏览一条消息,得知大意,如感兴趣再细读,否则就略过它。又如,在学习工作中,我们经常要查阅一些资料。查到资料后,首先要浏览了解文章大意,决定取舍。对于相关的文章或章节才细读。由此可见,快速捕捉文章大意是实用的阅读技能。

阅读下面短文了解文章大意。

There is Nothing Wrong with You

In the doctor's waiting room, the patients, men and women, old and young, were sitting quietly on the chairs, waiting their turns. Rod, a schoolboy, was sitting there, too. They all looked very sad except Rod. He was reading an interesting story in a magazine, and there was a smile on his face.

Just then the nurse came in to say the doctor was ready for the next patient. Rod jumped up and ran into the doctor's room.

"Good morning, doctor."

"Good morning. What's your trouble, young man?" asked the doctor. Before Rod could answer a word, the doctor made him lie down on a bed, "Now, let me listen to your heart." Rod tried to speak, but the doctor told him not to say anything. "I'll take your temperature." Rod tried to sit up, but the doctor stopped him. "Now open your mouth… Mm, good." After a moment, the doctor said, "Well, my boy, you haven't got a fever. It's nothing serious… Mm, in fact, there's nothing wrong with you."

"I know there isn't," said the boy. "I just came here to get some medicine for my father."

浏览上面的短文,不难获悉这是一个幽默的小故事:在医院门诊部候诊轮到一个小男孩进来,医生什么都没说马上给他量体温、听诊,最后发现孩子没有病,来医院是为生病的父亲抓药。故事属记叙文,是大家最熟悉的一种文体。记叙文一般是记叙过去发生的事,所以谓语动词常常用过去的时态。要想迅速捕捉文章大意,不必细读,即逐字逐行逐段地读,而应抓住记叙文的五大要素去浏览,即略读或跳读:When(时间)、Where(地点)、Who(人物)、What(事情)、Why(因果)。

(二)根据说明文和议论文的篇章结构线索增进阅读理解

说明文和议论文在篇章结构方面有共同的特点。这些特点在阅读理解过程中为我们提供了线索,使我们更快更好地理解词语、句子和整篇文章的意思,尤其在阅读较难懂的文章时。

1. 主题和子主题

每篇文章有一个明确的主题。主题作为文章的一条主线展开讨论。一篇文章可分为几个部分,每部分可分为若干节,每节可分为若干段落,每段包括若干句子。而每部分有子主题,每节有子主题,每段有子子主题。这些子主题、子子主题、子子子主题与文章的主题一致。对于有这种篇章结构的文章,我们通常评价说"文章主题明确,结构合理,层次清楚"。

需说明一点,上一段的讨论是指报刊常见的文章篇章结构,而本书所选的阅读文章,由于篇幅所限,都比较短,其中一些文章是节选的,不是完整的文章。尽管如此,了解文章的主题和子主题结构同样有助于理解本书所选的文章,试举一例。

阅读下面短文,分析文章的篇章结构。

Doctors say anger can be extremely damaging emotion, unless you learn how to deal with it. They warn that angry hostile feeling can lead to heart disease, stomach problems, headaches, emotional problems and possible cancer.

Anger is a normal emotion that we all feel from time to time. Some people express anger openly in a calm reasonable way. Others explode with anger, and yell. But other people keep their anger inside. They can not or will not express it. This is called repressing anger.

For years many doctors thought that repressing anger was more dangerous to a person's health than expressing it. They said that when a person is angry, the brain releases the same hormones that are produced during tense, stressful situations. These hormones speed the heart rate, raise blood pressure or sugar into the blood and narrow the blood vessels to the interstices. In general, the person feels excited and ready to act.

Doctors said that repressing these feelings and feelings to express the anger that caused them only make the feelings continue. And this can lead to many medical problems.

Some doctors said that both repressing and expressing anger and hostility can be dangerous.

Doctors say that a good way to deal with anger is to find humour in the situation that has made you angry. They say that laugher is much healthier than anger.

上面文章的篇章结构如下所示：

第1段文章主题：anger是一种伤人的情绪；

第2段子主题：人们对anger的应对方式不同；

第3段子主题：其中一类（repressing anger）有害健康；

第4段子主题：压抑自己的anger有害健康；

第5段子主题：压抑或发泄anger（对身体）都有害；

第6段子主题：幽默搞笑是应对anger的好办法。

2. 主题、子主题的位置

在例中，短文第1段的主题是该段的主题，同时也是文章的主题，即"生气有害于健康"。其余5段围绕此主题进行阐述。

文章的主题通常在文章的第1段阐明。因此，阅读第1段可以迅速把握文章的主题，捕捉文章大意，对于提高阅读质量十分有益。

如例所示，短文的每段都有一个子主题，表达此子主题的句子称为主题句。在典型的说明文或议论文中，主题句通常位于句首，如例中的第1、3—6段。然而，有时为了使文章不过于呆板，主题句的位置有些变化，如例中的第2段所示。

阅读每段时，找到主题句有助于捕捉该段大意，提高阅读速度。另外，在阅读中有时会发现某一段很难理解。在这种情况下，了解文章的主题以及其他各段的主题可以迅速破解该段的意思。

3. 段落内的篇章结构

在一般情况下，文章每段有一个子主题，有时几段共享一个子主题。通常段落的内部结构是：围绕该段的子主题，其他非主题句通过举例、对比、列举事实等阐述该子主题。也就是说，每段有一个主题句，该段的其余句子阐明这个主题。了解段落内部的这种句与句之间的关系可以提高阅读效率，尤其在阅读较难懂的文章时。

4. 标题

文章的大小标题也是篇章结构线索，利用此线索可以帮助我们了解文章大意和各段大意。

5. 语篇衔接

语篇衔接是指段与段、句与句之间的衔接。衔接手段包括表达各种逻辑关系的连接词语。遇到某一段费解时，可以读一读上一段末尾几句话，然后推断此段主要谈什么，因为在一般情况下，每段内容都是接着上段的话题继续谈。如转换话题，一般在段首要使用适当的连接词语指明。同样，遇到难句时，也可以借助句与句之间的衔接推断它的意思。

6. 首尾呼应

文章的首段一般为引言，尾段往往是归纳总结或下结论。通常，阅读首尾段可以获悉文章的主题和大意。

以上我们从六个方面谈了说明文和议论文的篇章结构线索。在阅读过程中，应根据具体情况同时使用一个或多个线索。

第五节　英语阅读中的其他策略

一、词语搭配线索

词语搭配是指词与词之间的组合,比如,"打电话"是动词与名词的组合,或称为动宾搭配。这种组合是相对固定的,是语言在长期使用中沿袭下来的搭配方式,不得随意改变。比如,"打"和"击"是同义词,但我们只能说"打电话",而不能说"击电话"。

偶尔会看到常用词语搭配的改变,往往为了搞笑或出于某些特定的意图,比如在做痔疮广告中出现的"有痔无恐",做"好记星"广告中见到的"好记星"表心愿,感动万千家长心。改变搭配是不规范的语言使用,因此也不多见。

在阅读过程中,借助词语搭配线索推测词语的意思是一种常用的阅读策略。在阅读文章中,常见的词语搭配关系有动词+名词、介词+名词、形容词+名词、冠词+名词、动词+副词、名词+动词等组合。例如:

(一)动词+名词

The sight of the mountains evoked memories of her childhood. (看到那些山 evoked 她对童年的回忆。)

根据 evoke 与 memories 的动宾搭配和上下文可以猜出 evoke 的意思为"引起,唤起"。

The man to whom we handed the forms pointed out that they had not been properly filled in.

A. consequently

B. thoroughly

C. regularly

D. correctly

答案为 D（correctly）。properly 意思是"适当的,正确的",与 correctly 意思相近。本句根据 point out（指出）与其后的宾语从句组成的动宾搭配线索可以推断词义。根据常识,"指出"一般都是指出填表中的错误,不妥之处。由此可推断四个选项中的 correctly 在意思上讲得通,而其他三个选项则讲不通：consequently 意思是"因而,所以"；thoroughly 意思是"完全"；regularly 意思是"有规律地,有规则地,整齐地,匀称地"。

特别指出一点,在例中有两个线索,（上一段谈的）point out＋that 从句是主要线索；另一个线索为动词与副词搭配（properly＋filled in）,是次要线索。在推断 properly 的意思时可用这两个线索,应以主要线索为主。

（二）形容词或名词等（作定语或同位语）＋名词

Becket was a professional traveler, interested and interesting. He liked to get the feeling of a place by living in it, reading its newspapers, watching its TV, discussing its affairs.

猜测 professional 的意思主要根据形容词（professional）与名词（traveler）的搭配关系。该词在文中的意思有两种可能性："专业的或业余的"。根据短文大意应取前者。

University freshman Zhen Zhen just had her photo taken without wearing any clothes, something she wants to see in the future to remind herself of those younger, former days.

The 19-year-old resident of southwest China's Chongqing city says that even though she did travel 500 kilometers to the Sichuan provincial capital Chengdu—where no one would know her—to pose for a local photographer, there's nothing wrong with nude photos, they aren't necessarily expensive, and it's not illegal.

本题主要根据 4 条线索推断词义：根据该词的定语 university 与其的搭配关系。又根据该词后面的同位语人名"珍珍",可以联想常见的搭配为"大学学生""大学教师""大学毕业生"等。另外,根据下一段第 1 句得知珍珍仅有 19 岁。常识告诉我们：7 岁上学,加上小学中学共 12 年,那么她多半是个大学低年级学生。由此可以排除另外两个搭配的可能性,即"大学教师"或"大学毕业生"。还有一个线索是词性线索：

第四章　英语阅读教学之学习策略探索

freshman 是一个合成词,由两部分组成,即 fresh 和 man。fresh 是"新鲜"的意思,加上前面的年龄线索,可推断珍珍可能是个新大学生。该词的意思是"大学一年级学生"。

二、经历、情景、常识线索

背景知识线索是指在阅读过程中,借助文章或句子中的上下文使人联想到某些相关的信息,如情景、常识、自己的经历、背景知识或语法知识。[①] 依据背景知识线索有助于阅读理解,是一种常用的阅读策略。

When Mr. Jones gets old, he will hand over his business to his son.(琼斯先生年老时要把他经营的买卖 hand over 给他的儿子。)

根据该句大意使人会联想起"子承父业"或"遗产继承",由此不难猜出 hand over 的意思是"移交,传给"。

The populace suffered terribly under the rule of the cruel king.(在国王的残酷的统治下,populace 遭受极大的痛苦。)

暴政猛于虎,遭殃的肯定是黎民百姓(populace)。

The spectators were not pleased with her performance.(spectators 对她的演出不满意。)

performance 一词使人联想起看节目演出的场景,在这种场合里主要参与者是演员和观众(spectators)。

The per capital income in the village was only two hundred dollars a year.(这个村子的 per capital 年收入仅有 200 元。)

根据常识,一个村子有多户人家,年收入 200 元不够养活一家人,此处该词语多半指"人均或每人"。

The age of a tree can be determined accurately by counting the number of tree rings it has developed.(通过计算树生长的年轮可以 determined 树的年龄。)

根据常识可以推断"rings 圈"是指树干的横断面上一圈一圈的年轮,由此不难猜出 determined 的词义为"确定"。

It is reported that most adopted children want to know who their

---

① 刘津开. 大学英语阅读策略训练[M]. 广州:华南理工大学出版社,2006.

natural parents are.（据报道，大多数 adopted 孩子都想知道他们的亲生父母是谁。）

根据常识和上下文很容易推测出该词的意思是"抱养的"。

三、语法知识线索

"Unfriendly" is an <u>antonym</u> for the word "friendly". （Unfriendly 是 friendly 的 antonym。）

根据构词法得知前缀"un-"表示否定，由此可推断 Unfriendly 与 friendly 的意思相反，因此可猜出 antonym 的大概意思为"意思相反的"。再根据语法知识，该词跟在冠词后，应是名词，那么它的词义应是"反义词"。

A Chinese exhibition of nude paintings in the mid-1980s stirred up the hottest debate ever over this branch of art. The husband of a woman who had modeled nude for some of the paintings <u>threatened</u> her with <u>divorce</u> when she was recognized by others in the pictures.

上例两个斜体单词是生词，要求猜测它们的意思。猜测它们的词义首先要了解本段大意：有一个画展举办。一个女人做过裸体模特，丈夫说过什么"如果要被人认出来将如何如何"。根据语法知识，可以确定 threatened 是动词，divorce 是名词。由此可推断后者可能是"离婚"，前者或许是说过什么威胁的话。另外，了解句子的语法结构，比如独立主格结构、介词短语、分词短语等用于表示原因、伴随状态等，有助于提高我们的阅读理解能力。

第五章　英语阅读教学中的方法掌握探索

一说到教学法，人们往往只想到教法，而很少想到学法。实际上教学法应该既包括教法，又包括学法。教法是指教师教学活动的方法，学法是指学生进行学习活动的方法。本章重点研究英语阅读教学中的方法掌握。

第一节　阅读方法简述

一、关于阅读和阅读方法的概述

近现代名人学者们通过大量有效的阅读，积累了丰富的知识，形成了宝贵的思想，成为阅读的典范。他们提炼出各自不同的方法，是当今读者学习的榜样。马克思的"博采法"——用博采聚集知识，博而精、精而究的方法；毛泽东的"四多"法——多读、多思、多写、多问的方法；鲁迅的"跳读"法；爱因斯坦的"总、分、合"法；杨振宁的"渗透"法；老舍的"印象"法；杰克·伦敦的"饿狼式"法；白寿彝的"研读"法；毛姆的"乐趣"法；余秋雨的"畏友"法；朱熹的"循序渐进"法；华罗庚的"厚薄"法；郑板桥的"攻探学问"（"攻"谓之"破"，理解透彻；"问"，不耻下问，问遍可问之人）法，等等。

二、阅读和理解策略

什么叫策略？策略的英文为 strategy，指的是计策、谋略、对策、行动计划（见《21世纪大英汉词典》），或为实现目标所采取的一系列思维和行为步骤（《有道桌面词典》）。① 策略主要表现为实现某一目标的方案集合，具体体现在方案的多样化和应变能力上。所谓阅读策略，根据丹塞路（Dansereau，1985）和迈克卡（Mckeachie，1990）给学习策略的定义的原理，我们不妨把阅读策略定义为直接操作阅读材料的各种手段、措施和方法，包括信息获得、储存、检索和应用等。阅读策略还包括元认知策略——读者为获取适当阅读氛围，进行计划制订和时间规划、注意力分配所采取的手段、措施和方法等。

（一）阅读的策略

一是定向阅读。人生有涯知无涯，要把人生宝贵的时间用于有明确目的的阅读，才会收到应有的效果。

二是有选择地阅读。世上有各种各样的书，有的根本不值得一看。选择性阅读含义有二：一为"读第一流的书"，二为"读一流学者写的书"。弗朗西斯·培根说过："一些书需浅尝，一些书需生吞，仅少数的书需嚼烂消化。"

三是时间巧安排。利用上课、上班时间，阅读与学习和工作有关的书籍、文章；利用课余或工余时间，根据自己的兴趣和需要，广泛涉猎，大量阅读，多读书、读好书。

（二）理解的策略

理解的策略，概括起来讲，有八点：丰富背景知识、新旧对接、置疑、心图、推测、总结、评价、综合。

---

① 周荣辉. 英语阅读理解策略与技巧[M]. 成都：西南交通大学出版社，2009.

(1)丰富读者阅读前的知识(Enriching prior knowledge)。

(2)阅读与联系(Reading & making a connection)。将在读文本与经历、其他书或关于世界的其他事实联系起来。(Relating a passage to an experience, another book, or other facts about the world.)

(3)质疑(Questioning)。Dr. Neil Postman曾经说过:"我们的全部知识都源于质疑。"(All our knowledge results from questions.)

(4)形象化(Visualization)。阅读时,在脑海中创设图像或影像,就如"心像"一样。(Creating a picture or movie in mind while reading text like a mental image.)

(5)推理(Inferring)。根据文本线索探究出真实含义。(Figuring out what it really means from clues in the text.)

(6)总结(Summarizing)。总结就是讲述文本的重点,应包括谁、什么、哪里、何时、为何和如何的答案。(Summarizing is telling what is important about the text. A summary might include the answers to who, what, where, when, why, and how.)

(7)评价(Evaluation)。要对所读做出判断,并说明判断的依据。(Evaluation is about making judgments on what you read and then explaining why you made those judgments (into the book).)

(8)重构(Synthesizing)。将重点和要点以新的方式重新组合起来。(Putting the pieces together to see them in a new way.)

三、英语阅读的主要方法

英语阅读的方法很多,主要方法可概括为七种:整体阅读法、三阶段阅读法、三层次阅读法、三层面阅读法、八步阅读法和五步阅读法、7T阅读法以及提纲式阅读法。

(一)整体阅读法

整体阅读法(Total Reading Method)是从阅读材料的整体出发,采用"从整体入手—分解导读—再回归整体"的三段式阅读法,爱因斯坦把它概括为"总—分—合"阅读法。它是阅读的基本方法之一,其阅读的过程可分为"整体感知—具体分析—总结深化"三个环节。

(二)三阶段阅读法

三阶段阅读法(The Three-stage Reading Method)包括预览(Previewing)或预读(Pre-reading)、阅读(While-reading)和后读(Post-reading)三步骤。

在此仅以英文的论述为例加以阐释,使大家进一步加深理解。此阅读法既适用于书籍的阅读,也适用于文章的阅读。

1. 预览/预读(Previewing/Pre-reading before Starting Reading)

Look through the relevant parts of the potential text to assure the general understanding of it by answering the following questions.

Is this the correct book/article for your purpose? Check date/author/scope, scan the contents.

Is it the right level? Read a section/chapter to check.

What questions are you trying to answer?

Clarify the contents mentioned before you start.

General beginning questions（读前一般性的问题）:

One logical way of starting out is to pose a few simple questions from the list below as you begin any new reading. Depending on the kind of reading or the context of the reading, you might not always ask all these questions. Soon, however, the questions you ask regularly will become part of the way you approach all readings. The following questions are worthwhile to consider:

• What do I know about this author? Has anything been mentioned so far in class or in other readings which gives me a hint about what to expect from this author?

• When was this piece of text written? Does that time suggest any contextual information which will help me understand the material or think critically about it? (For example, a title such as "Equality in the Workplace" might be interpreted one way if it were written in 1967 and possibly suggest different issues if it were written in 1995.)

• At what point in my course does this reading come? What might I expect this reading to contribute to the development of the main concepts or themes in my course? Why am I reading this? Is it for class discussion? For an essay? To review for an exam?

• What structures can I rely on: introductions, summaries, chapter goals, headings, sub-headings, key words, glossaries, graphs, charts, photos and other visual aids?

2. 正读(While-reading)

Read with purpose (what questions to be answered).

Read selectively—scan and skim, only read in detail what you need to. Mentally recite what you have just read.

Make notes at appropriate points-bullet points, do not rewrite the whole book.

3. 后读(Post-reading/Reviewing)

Some suggested questions to ask and answer after reading:
Did I answer the questions I wanted to?
Do I understand and remember what I read?
How well do I understand this reading?
Have I been able to construct a reasonable meaning for this reading?
What questions do I have regarding parts that are unclear?
What are my difficulties? Where can I go for help? What could correct this situation?
What is different between the structure of this reading and what I want to learn?
What is the relationship of this material to other materials or the relationship among parts of this reading?

(三)三层次阅读

三层次阅读(Three Levels of Reading)是指字面阅读,推理性阅读和批判/评价性阅读(Literal Reading,Inferential Reading and Critical/Evaluative Reading)。

(1)字面阅读指的是读懂作者直接陈述的观点和事实,是最基础、最简单的表层阅读。英文阅读理解涉及语篇、段落、句子、词汇四个层次的理解问题,而其中最基本的是对词汇的理解。词汇是构成语言的基本元素。如果掌握的词汇量太小,读一篇文章,处处是生词,则会举步维艰,文章不可能顺利读懂。而阅读理解的关键又在于读懂文章。[1]

(2)推理性阅读指的是读懂作者没有直接陈述的观点,是一种较难的、更复杂的阅读。它包括"部分—整体—相关问题"(part-whole-connection questions)的过程。推理性阅读通常需要回答以下两类问题:特殊疑问句问题和假设性问题。

特殊疑问句(Wh-questions)。

- How … ?
- Why … ?
- What are the reasons for … ?
- What the types of … ?
- What are the functions of … ?
- What is the process of … ?
- What are the causes/results of … ?
- What is the relationship between … and … ?
- What is the similarity or difference between … and … ?
- How does … apply to … ?
- What are the problems or conflicts or issues associated with … ?
- What are possible solutions/resolutions to these problems or conflicts or issues … ?
- What is the main argument or thesis of … ?
- How is this argument developed … ?
- What evidence or proof or support is offered … ?
- What are other theories arguments from other authors … ?

---

[1] 李杰.英语阅读方法学习与能力训练[M].青岛:青岛海洋大学出版社,2001.

假设性问题(Hypothesis Questions)。
- If … occurs, then what happens … ?
- If … had happened, then what would be different … ?
- What does theory x predict will happen … ?

(3)批判/评价性阅读是一种主动的、创造性的阅读技巧。它要求读者对阅读材料提出质疑、进行比较和评价。好的读者能读懂文章未直接陈述而隐含的意思。

批判/评价性问题常见的有:
- good or bad … ?
- correct or incorrect … ?
- effective or ineffective … ?
- relevant or irrelevant … ?
- clear or unclear … ?
- logical or illogical … ?
- applicable or not applicable … ?
- proven or not proven … ?
- ethical or unethical … ?
- What are the advantages or disadvantages of … ?
- What are the pros or cons of … ?
- What is the best solution to the problem/conflict/issue … ?
- What should or should not happen … ?
- Do I agree or disagree … ?
- What is my opinion … ?
- What is my support for my opinion … ?

上述三类问题是专门为检测阅读过程中是否读懂原文(著)而设计的。针对某一阅读文本,只需回答与之有关的问题,无需回答所有问题。若读者能回答那些相关问题,就说明读懂了;若只能回答部分问题,就说明只是部分读懂。一般的阅读要求和目标是前者。

(四)三层面阅读法

三层面阅读法包括英语文章阅读的三个层面:超段落阅读(Reading beyond Paragraphs)、句段阅读(Reading within Paragraphs and Sentences)、利用词语的呼应关系阅读(Reading with Coherence of Words and Phrases)。此阅读法主要针对文章的阅读。

(1)超段落阅读,意为把握该篇文章的整体内容和主旨,了解段与段之间的逻辑关系及段落大意,并联想其他经历或其他文章的内容。

(2)句段阅读,意为在同一段落中把握句子之间和句子内的结构、逻辑关系和内在联系,包括句内语序、句子成分以及语义的理解。

(3)利用词语的呼应关系阅读,意为利用词语的呼应关系理解陌生词语及句子的意思,读懂字面意思和隐含意思,把握词与词之间的内在联系。

(五)八步阅读法(PSQ5R)

八步阅读法是一种阅读模式,它代表了通过阅读有效地学习的基本步骤。其中,P 表示 Purpose(目的),S 表示 Survey(浏览),Q 表示 Question(置疑),5R 包括 Reading Selectively(选择性阅读)、Reciting(复述)、Reducing-record(关键词语提要法)、Reflecting(反思)和 Reviewing(复习)。

1. 目的

阅读前读者需有明确的阅读目的,即读者到底想从阅读材料中获取什么。阅读目的一旦实现,阅读也就完成了。比如,在电话号码簿中查找某人的电话号码,这个目的单一又清楚,一旦找到了该号码,此次阅读随即终止。这样的阅读非常快捷,可能达到每分钟十万字。这种阅读或许可以叫作"扫读"。只有阅读方法与目的一致时,阅读才会快捷、高效。阅读之前树立明确的目的,即掌握文本讨论的焦点、主题或中心思想、主要的事实、数据、证据、议论、例证、关联或方法,才能使你用最短的时间达到阅读目的。

2. 浏览

浏览文本的主要部分,如标题、小标题、引入语和段落总结等,以达到总览全文,找出文中讨论的观点、难点和需要解决的问题的目的。要达到这个目的,读者需要把握文章的焦点或主题,或许还需要了解作者使用的方法和手段,而整个浏览过程只需一两分钟。

3. 置疑

置疑就是写出你需要回答的问题。

(1) 对这个主题你了解多少,换言之,就是激活背景知识。

(2) 把标题变成一个问句,阅读时你会去寻找答案。比如,将"The effects of the Hundred Years' War"变成"What were the effects of the Hundred Years' War?"。读者可能写出"On democracy, or on the economy?"或"What is the impact of unions on wages?"等问题。

4. 选读

阅读查找答案。阅读每段的第一句或许就能找到答案。有时文章会以这种方式罗列答案"The first point … Secondly …"等。有时得认真阅读每一段才能读懂下一段的内容,理解深藏其间的焦点、中心思想等。总之,找到观点、信息、证据等,才能达到阅读的目的。

5. 复述

复述意为不看原文,尽可能用自己的话回答提出的问题。如果做不到这一点,需要再回去读那部分。

6. 关键词提要法

关键词提要法是将读者提出的问题和找到的答案以提纲的方式列出来。问题的答案需用关键词语,不需使用长句。比如"Effects of 100 Years' War? —Consolidate Fr. King's power."或"Unions on Wages?"。提纲的内容一般仅占原文的10%—15%。

7. 反思

认知心理学的最新研究表明,当你认真领会新的信息时,你会获得新的理解和收获。这就是反思已经阅读过的内容,即对阅读材料进行比较、分类,改变其表达方式,与同文的其他部分进行联系,与其他知识或个人经历进行联系等。一句话,将原文内容进行新的排列组合,可以采用思维的方式或以书面形式写出来等。也可采用关键词提要法的方法,列出正式的提纲,分出层次、目录、图表,甚至可以随手涂鸦,然后按照上述第 3—7 步的方法再过一遍。

8. 复习

复习是把浓缩的笔记从头至尾地浏览一遍,这有利于回忆整个文本的结构和内容,或者口头回答所提出的问题,或根据其他提纲式的线索词表述其内容。后一种复述可以在几分钟内完成。运用此法可将一两周内已阅读的重要内容复习一遍。

(六)五步阅读法(SQ3R)

五步阅读法是由美国依阿华大学创造的,后来流行在英美等国的一种综合性读书法。SQ3R 的 S 表示 Survey(浏览),Q 表示 Question(提问),R 表示 Reading(阅读),R 表示 Reciting(复述),R 表示 Reviewing(复习)。这种阅读方法主要是针对书籍的阅读,当然也适合于文章的阅读。该法将阅读过程分为五个步骤,与上述的八步阅读法有相似之处,属于"整体阅读法(Total Reading Method)"的范畴。

1. 浏览

这一步骤与前面的预览/预读(Previewing/Pre-reading)相同。通过阅览前言、序跋、目录、内容、摘要及正文中的大小标题、注释、附录等,概要性地把书浏览一遍,对全书有个整体印象,把握书的重点和难点。

2. 发问

对书中的重点和难点进行提问,以便在深层阅读理解中进行思考,以寻求答案。古人云:"为学患无疑,疑则有进。"这话点明了做学问让人担心的是提不出问题,读书或做学问必须质疑,有疑问才能有进步。

3. 阅读

带着所提的问题,对阅读材料进行深入细致的阅读,并做好笔记,以加深理解和增强记忆。

4. 复述

在阅读理解的基础上,对阅读中所获取的知识和信息进行回忆,检查重点是否掌握、难点是否突破,以提高阅读的效果。

5. 复习

对阅读过的内容不断地进行复习,以巩固记忆,保证学习成果。

五步阅读法符合感知、记忆与思维相联系的认知心理规律,因而是一种行之有效的读书方法。

(七)7T 阅读法

7T—Title/Heading,Subtitle/Subheading,Theme,Type,Topic,Tone,Style(标题、副标题、主题、体裁、主题句、语气和风格)。7T 阅读也可分为三个层面:第一层面包括前 4T(Title/Heading,Subtitle/Subheading,Theme,Type),主旨是贯彻整体把握文章的中心和主题,与其他方法不同的是加入了 Type(体裁),原因是基于体裁不同结构相异,分清体裁在阅读理解中也是非常重要的;第二层面是要在阅读中重点把握主题句(Topic),各段的主题句是整篇文章主题的重要组成部分,只要抓住了各部分的主题句,整篇文章的中心内容就已在把握中,至于细节可等到需要时再读不迟;第三层面包括语气(Tone)和风格(Style),这是对文章的鉴赏和分析,语气和风格的赏析可以提高对文章的深层理解。

(八)提纲式阅读法

无论是写作还是阅读,提纲都能给读者一个清晰的思路。通过提纲,在写作时检查是否按原来的思路在展开,在阅读时可以检查是否按照作者的思路来理解,这对读者是非常重要的。当你在阅读一篇文章时,理清作者的写作思路,可以迅速把握作者的中心思想和文本的结构特点。下面是一份建议性的报告文的提纲,由此可以明白如何拟出文章的提纲。

Christmas in Mexico (The title)

Introduction

Thesis (Purpose statement): The purpose of this paper is to define what Christmas is, explain how it is celebrated in some parts of Mexico, and describe some typical Christmas foods associated with it.

Body

(Paragraph 1)

Topic Sentence: Studying the definition of the word "Christmas" can help us understand the background behind this holiday.

Supporting Sentences:

Christmas, coming from Old English "Cristes maesse" or "Christ's mass", is a celebration of the nativity of Jesus Christ.

Celebrations of the winter solstice in the Northern hemisphere have been a time of rejoicing among many ancient cultures.

The reason for celebrating Christmas on December 25th is still unclear.

(Paragraph 2)

Topic Sentence: Cultural traditions have had an influence on the Christmas celebrations of today in Mexico.

Supporting Sentences:

The celebration of the winter solstice in Mexico even proceeded with the arrival of the Spanish who brought Christianity with them.

One of the oldest traditional events in Mexico, Las Posadas (meaning "lodgings").

Other non-religious activities are also held during that season including parades and pinatas.

(Paragraph 3)

Topic Sentence: In addition to Christmas activities, many food dishes are served during this period.

Supporting Sentences:

Perhaps the most popular of all Christmas foods in Mexico are tamales.

Other pastries are also eaten as well.

Conclusion

As you can see from my paper, Christmas is important in the lives of the Mexican people.

阅读实践训练:

以短文 Sandra Brown Williams 为例,阅读并拟出文章提纲。

Sandra Brown Williams (The title)

Thesis (Purpose Statement): The purpose of this story is to introduce one of the most interesting female literary figures of the century, Sandra Brown Williams.

(Paragraph 1)

Topic Sentence: This story concerns one of the most interesting female literary figures of the century, Sandra Brown Williams.

Supporting Sentences:

1. She is a profile writer… the most significant novelist to have emerged in the last fifty years. Her lively imagination has led her to create five main novels, thirty-three poems, dozens of essays, and six plays.

2. Miss Williams has attempted to paint an overall view of the world where people from all walks of life suffer silent tragedies and join hands to form a single but broad picture of reality.

(Paragraph 2)

Topic Sentence: Miss Williams's background of the society and family.

Supporting Sentences:

1. (She was) born during the last years of the Depression in a town where many failed to finish grammar school.

2. In fact, her father received no formal education at all.

3. She was close to her mother, an enterprising woman who painted intricate miniatures… In the background, her father played the violin and the cello by ear during the few free hours away from his business. (good influence from her parents)

(Paragraph 3)

Topic Sentence: A trip to a nearby aunts house introduced the young girl to the agonies of existence.

Supporting Sentences：

1. She watched her mother's sister died of cancer over a period of ten months.

2. She found her uncle's body after he had committed suicide due to his wife's agonizing death.

3. These experiences left a strong mark on her tender and creative mind.

(Paragraph 4)

Topic Sentence：She was successful in writing and lived happily in her later life.

Supporting Sentences：

1. Sandra Brown Williams entered Bucknell University in 1951 at the age of sixteen.

2. She continued to write. She was awarded the Marks Prize for literature in 1953.

3. She attended graduate school at Collins University in Pittsburgh.

4. She met her future husband, Anthony Wright Daniels, on January 5,1954. A month later they were married.

5. Sandra acquired a job in the English Department at Collins.

第二节 影响阅读效果的要素

阅读效果的优劣与两大要素有关：语言要素和非语言要素。语言要素指语言知识和有关语言交际的知识；非语言要素指信息加工策略要素、文化背景知识和智力要素。下面分别逐一说明。

一、语言要素

在一般英语阅读中，我们总是先弄清楚每个由不同字母组合成的单

词的意思,然后弄清楚每个词与其他词的关系,也就是每个词在句子中所起的语法作用。例如:

Don't expect to find an easy way to learn.

宾语中 an easy way 又作 find 的宾语,不定式 to learn 是 way 的定语。全句为祈使句,意思是"别指望学习有捷径。"因此,词汇和语法是阅读的先决条件,即阅读最基本的要素。但是碰到下面的句子,每个词都认识,可不一定能看懂句子:

I'm not as far along as I'd like to be, but at least I'm on the right track.

其实,如能知道 as far along as(远至)、I'd like(我真希望)和 at least(至少)3 个短语的意思,就能看懂全句了:我没有达到我预期的目标,但至少我所走的路是对的。英语中各种短语成千上万,如果没有短语知识的积累,同样难以进行流畅的阅读。

有了词汇、语法、短语知识还不够,还要有弄清楚句与句之间关系的能力,即能判断句子间的逻辑关系,理解句内语义关系,段内语义关系和篇章语义关系。请看:

①That's not to say everyone needs re-invent the wheel. ②Textbooks and language learning programs can provide a useful service. ③ I started learning Chinese with a textbook. ④ Crazy English may work great for you. ⑤Most language education is based on the reality ⑥that people are people, ⑦that we have some things in common, ⑧that we learn in similar ways, ⑨so what works for me might work, at least partly, for you. ⑩But each of us is also unique, ⑪so know yourself and make your study methods suit you.

在这一小段中②、③、④和⑤句之间的逻辑关系是什么?⑤、⑥、⑦和⑧句之间是什么关系?⑩和⑪句与全段是什么关系?

前文作者提出要以成功者为榜样走自己的路,本处进一步坦言走自己的路并不是要每个人去重新发明车轮,也就是说教科书还是有用的,③句作为一个例证,④句对"疯狂英语"加以肯定,⑤、⑥、⑦和⑧句进一步从理论上论证。⑥、⑦和⑧句形成并列关系,都是 reality 的同位语从句,或者说是三个理论依据。⑨句为作者的结论,⑩和⑪句又回到前文的主题——走自己的路,预示下文将详细讨论反映个性差异的学习方法。全段各句之间的关系可描述为:承上(①)——本段主题(②)——论证主题(③、④、⑤、⑥、⑦和⑧)——本段结论(⑨)——启下(⑩和⑪)。

由此可知,阅读不仅需要词汇、语法、短语知识,更要从段落篇章角度理解作者的观点、态度,这样才能达到阅读的目的。

二、非语言要素

(一)信息加工策略要素

国内外一些专家对信息加工策略作了许多研究,共同之处可归纳为以下几点。

1. 能用自己掌握的有关外在世界的知识和语言知识预测和解释所读材料

所谓预测,就是利用我们已积累的各类知识对作者将要传递的信息做出预见,比如读到 Mr. White 短文的标题"How Can I Improve My English?",我们自然想知道他提出的学习方法和自己的有什么相同或不同。但读到第 2 段(It seems a perfectly fair and simple question, and it's a question I hate.)时,你有没有做出预测?看到 seems 和 hate 时你预测作者是回答还是不回答这个问题?毫无疑问作者是要回答的,但他的用词告诉我们:下面的回答很可能不是提问者所需要的答案。果然,在第 5 段他直截了当地说:"Oh, I have answers, and I stumble around in my response, hoping the students won't notice how unsure I am. I have answers, but I don't have the answer, not the answer I think they're looking for."如此看来,预测实际上是读者和作者就某一话题在进行无声的对话。

2. 能迅速对语篇中阐述的细节分清主要信息和次要信息、整体和部分关系、陈述与例释关系、观点与事实关系

请看下面两段,试说明句中主要信息和次要信息、整体和部分、陈述与例释、观点与事实等各种关系。

Find your own success story. Remember, people like U Yang are

第五章　英语阅读教学中的方法掌握探索

only successful now because they found their own way to study English; they figured out a method that works best for them. Now they are trying to make you follow the trail they have blazed when what you should be doing is following their example by blazing your own trail.

That's not to say everyone needs re-invent the wheel. Textbooks and language learning programs can provide a useful service. I started learning Chinese with a textbook. Crazy English may work great for you. Most language education is based on the reality that people are people, that we have some things in common, that we learn in similar ways, so what works for me might work, at least partly, for you. But each of us is also unique, so know yourself and make your study methods suit you.

文中第1句"Find your own success story",和结束语"know yourself and make your study methods suit you"前后呼应:语言学习很重要的是找出适合自己的学习方法,这是成功之路。这是作者给英语学习者提出的建议或者说是忠告。当然这是文中的主要信息(primary information),也是作者的观点。

第2句 people…successful 与…now because they found their own way to study English; they figured out a method that works best for them. Now they are trying to make you follow the trail they have blazed…各句属于陈述(statement)与例释(examples)的关系,people…successful 陈述一个事实,其余各句则解释他们成功的原因以及对他人的榜样作用。(注意:when 的意思是"此时",全句意为"此时你要做的,则是以他们为榜样,走出你自己辉煌的路。")第2段中的(Textbooks and language learning programs…useful service)教科书和学习教程十分有用是作者的意见、看法(opinion),接着列出两个事例:"I started learning Chinese with a text-book."和"Crazy English may work great for you."。然后从理论高度说明教科书和学习教程存在的合理性以及学习方法的可借鉴性。所以,"Most language education is based on the reality that people are people, that we have some things in common, that we learn in similar ways, so what works for me might work, at least partly, for you."各句属于事实(facts)。

阅读中迅速分清主要信息和次要信息、整体和部分关系、陈述与例释关系、观点与事实关系,是非常重要的信息加工策略,它能帮助我们加深对文章的理解,提高阅读速度。

(二)文化背景知识要素

众所周知,任何一种语言都有滋养其产生和发展的文化土壤,不同的文化,造就不同的语言。因此,对于学外语的人来说,了解所学语言的文化知识是非常重要的。而且,汉语与英语又分属于截然不同的两个语系——东方语系和印欧语系。这两种语言在文化上,无论是历史文化、区域文化还是宗教文化方面都存在很大的差异。如果不了解这些差异,有时很难与西方人交流。像我们挂在嘴边的表示谦虚的"哪里,哪里"在英美人那里根本听不到。如果美国人说"Your wife is very purity.",我们常会回答"哪里,哪里"。反过来,如果我们对美国人说"Your wife is very party.",他们不仅不会说"No,just so-so.",而且会很认真地告诉你她哪个地方漂亮,甚至告诉你,那是他最欣赏的地方。同样,文化背景知识对于正确理解文章内容起着很大的作用。如读到"Santa Claus can't put a pony into a stocking."和"He couldn't lead a pony down the chimney either."这样两句话时,也许会问Santa Claus(圣诞老人)是谁?为什么说床头的袜子装不下一头小马?小马也不能从烟筒进到屋子里面来?现在我们接触西方文化多了,对这样一个古老的圣诞节故事有所了解了,也就能理解过节的孩子们纯真和迫切得到礼物的心情。①

再如,"It's normally hard to turn her away as it is hard to turn away a lost dog,turn a lost dog away from your door."这句中的"dog"为什么不能被赶走呢? 其实,在西方的社会习俗中,狗被当作心爱的东西和忠实的朋友。英国国王爱德华七世驾崩后,其爱犬走在送葬队伍的前头。著名的奥地利作曲家莫扎特与世长辞时,唯有他忠实的狗随灵柩来到墓地。因此,英语中有big dog(最重要的人物),lucky dog(幸运儿)之类的说法。回到刚才那句,如果将走失了的狗赶走是有违习俗的,当然是万万不可的,更何况一个无家可归的老人呢!

学习语言的人越来越感到了解西方文化的必要性。这一点也受益

---

① 周荣辉.英语阅读理解策略与技巧[M].成都:西南交通大学出版社,2009.

第五章 英语阅读教学中的方法掌握探索

于语言学家们的研究成果。在20世纪70年代中后期,社会语言学的研究掀起了高潮。澳大利亚的韩礼德认为对语言的描述应包括三个层次,即声音、形式(语法、词汇)和语用。

霍尔(Hall)在 *Beyond Culture* 一文中提出跨文化交际(intercultural communication)。从"文化休克"到第二语言习得中"文化融入"现象的研究,揭示了语言、文化、语言习得、语言课堂教学之间的内在联系,告诉我们语言习得(学习)过程是熟悉了解大写的 Culture(包括文学、艺术、音乐、建筑、哲学和科技成就等人类文明的各个方面)的过程,也是熟悉了解小写的 culture(包括人们的风俗、生活方式、行为准则、社会组织相互关系的文化特征)的过程。简言之,就是要了解西方文化中代表人类文明的各个方面,就是要了解西方人(主要是英美人)是怎么想事的,即他们的思维逻辑,及其如何反映到语言即表达方式上的。请看下面的短文:

We buried Donald Brown last May. He was murdered by four men who wanted to rob the supermarket manager he was protecting. Patrolman Brown was 61 years old. In just six months he and his wife had planned to retire to Florida. Now there will be no retirement in the sun, and she is alone.

Donald Brown was the second police officer to die since I became Police Commissioner of Boston in 1972. The first was Detective John Schroeder, shot in a pawnshop (当铺) robbery in November 1970. John Schroeder was the brother of Walter Schroeder, who was killed in a bank robbery in 1970. Their names are together on the honor roll in Police Headquarters.

At least two of these police officers were shot by a handgun, the kind almost anyone can buy nearly everywhere for a few dollars. Ownership of handguns has become so widespread that this weapon is no longer merely the instrument of crime; it is now a cause of violent crime. Of the 11 Boston police officers killed since 1962, seven were killed with handguns; of the 18 wounded by guns since 1962, 17 were shot with handguns.

Gun advocates are fond of saying that guns don't kill, people do. But guns do kill. Half of the people who commit suicide do so with handguns, Fifty-four percent of the murders committed in 1972 were committed with handguns.

No one can convince me, after returning from patrolman Brown's funeral, that we should allow people to own handguns. I know that many Americans feel deeply and honestly that they have a right to own and enjoy guns. I am asking that they give them up. I am not asking for registration or licensing, or the outlawing of cheap guns. I am saying that no private citizen, whatever his claim, should possess a handgun. Only police officers should.

这是一篇有关美国人枪支持有情况及其产生的严重后果——警察也未能幸免于难——的短文。在短文最后，警察呼吁要禁枪，说明在美国禁枪是件难事。这样的话题可能令我们中国人大感不解，又令我们中国人感到恐怖。我们自然要问：美国人干吗要拥有那么多枪支啊？既然那么多无辜的人死于枪口之下，为什么政府不禁止私人拥有枪支？在提出这样的问题时，实际上我们正在了解美国大写和小写的culture，因为这涉及美国人的习俗、生活方式、行为准则、社会政治制度、社会组织相互关系等方面的历史和现状。我们大概都看过美国的西部风情片，对西部牛仔的形象或许有印象：牛仔帽、枪和骏马。请看：

The American cowboy first appeared in Texas around 1836. Soon ranches（农场）spread and cowboys were working in almost every part of the West.

Cowboys' lives centered around the roundup（赶拢家畜等）and the cattle drive. Every winter and summer the cattle fed at the ranch. In the spring and autumn the cowboys rounded up the cattle, and separated the beef cattle from the rest of the herd, and drove them over many miles of open country to the nearest railroad station. From there the cattle were sent to slaughterhouses（屠宰场）. In the 19th century, rail-roads were few and far between. Driving the cattle was a long hard job. There was danger from cattle thieves. The cowboys rose at sun-up to start the cattle moving. They drove them all day through the heat or dust or wind. The men were often on horseback 15 hours a day. Cowboys had to be skillful and strong. They had to be skilled horsemen and good gunmen. Their clothing was made for protection. The wide-brimmed（宽沿

第五章 英语阅读教学中的方法掌握探索

的）hat was worn to protect them from the sun, the dust and the rain. The gun protected them against cattle thieves.

牛仔的生活方式构成了美国文化中最靓丽的风景线。请看：

People think of cowboys as free people, unafraid to battle with wild animals, living close to nature, with the trees and the sky and the stars. Today there are far fewer cowboys, and they no longer live as they did. But their influence on the imagination is still strong. The old-time cowboys is the hero of many books, films and songs. He is a national hero and a treasured part of the national past.

由此便知，牛仔被视为民族英雄，他们及他们的生活方式被视为国家历史珍贵的组成部分，这无疑极大地影响美国人的习俗、生活方式和行为准则。将本文和关于枪的短文联系起来，我们就知道在美国禁枪难的原因了。就是普通美国人在参加投票时，在他们所考虑的广泛问题中，很少考虑枪支控制问题（In the broad range of issues that most American voters consider when they go to vote, gun control might seldom be taken into account.），加之美国的竞选制度，如果候选人说了一些反对持枪的话，那些狂热的拥护持枪的人肯定会投他的反对票，不管他在其他问题上的立场如何（The Republican candidate say something negative about guns and these gun-owners will certainly vote against him on election day, no matter what his position is on other issues.）。如果控枪问题在竞选中出现，全美枪支协会的成员会将其视为"焦点"问题，持枪族们会成为"单一问题投票者"，严重破坏社会的立法（For many NRA members, if gun control comes up in an election campaign, it automatically becomes the "issue". Gun fanatics are perfect examples of "single-issue voters" who can seriously damage law-making in a society…）

以上告诉我们，如果对所学语言国家的文化有所了解的话，我们对相关文章的理解一是会变得容易，二是会更加深刻。请完成本短文练习：

1. The suggestion the author presents in the passage is that _____.

A. handguns are the cause of violent crime

B. handguns are a dangerous weapon

C. American people's right to own and enjoy guns should be respected

D. only police officers should possess guns

2. In paragraph 1, the tone of the author is _____.

A. calm B. bitter

C. exciting D. regretful

3. When did the author become Police Commissioner of Boston?

A. In 1972. B. In November, 1970.

C. In 1962. D. Before 1970.

4. According to the author, which is true of handguns?

A. They don't kill.

B. We should not allow people to own handguns.

C. Anyone can easily buy a handgun at a very high price.

D. Handguns can't be the cause of violent crime.

5. The passage is mainly aimed to _____.

A. persuade the government

B. describe police officers death

C. tell the robbers' means to kill policeman

Dexplain means of people's possession of guns

【答案】1. A 2. D 3. A 4. B 5. A

(三)智力要素

智力要素中逻辑思维能力是语言学习能力的基础。一般来说，人对语言的理解过程是由感知(听看)开始，进入形象思维，再进入抽象逻辑思维，最后获得信息。这个过程是一种新的代替旧的，由低级变成较高一级层次的发展过程。如果学习者止步于形象思维，没有向高层次的逻辑思维发展，也就无法理解事物的内在本质和规律性。语言学习也是如此。智力要素中语言观察能力是使所有语言学习能力产生作用的前提。

第五章　英语阅读教学中的方法掌握探索

第三节　阅读技能的训练

一、快速高效阅览的策略

根据不同的阅读目的和阅读材料选择合适的阅览模式、技巧和方法。比如,要了解甲型 H1N1 流感疫情的最新情况,如感染人数、地域、疫苗的研制实验情况等,收看中央电视台 1、4、9 频道的新闻播报,上互联网查询甲型 H1N1 流感(Swine Flu),均可获得大量最新的信息。如果要查寻"提高英语听力技巧",可直接输入要查寻的关键词,网上有相当多的相关内容可供阅读。①

二、利用上下文线索

(一)利用上下文猜测生词

充分利用上下文给出的线索,可以猜测大多数生词的意思。
下面介绍一些利用上下文猜测生词的基本方法。
(1)利用定义线索猜测生词词义。
(2)利用同义线索猜测生词词义。
(3)利用反义线索猜测生词词义。
(4)利用常识猜测生词词义。
(5)利用等式或符号猜测生词词义。

---

① 郭浩儒.大学英语阅读学习方法指导和技能训练[M].北京:宇航出版社,2001.

(二)利用标志词判断语义

充分利用标志词表示的句段前后的逻辑关系判断语义。

(1)并列关系的标志词,如 and, as well as, for, not only … but also 等。

(2)转折关系的标志词,如 but, however 等。

(3)时间事件顺序关系的标志词,如 first, second, at last, in the end 等。

三、计时阅读

阅读时要计时,或者有一个大致的时间计划。消遣性的阅读除外。与此同时,不要忽视理解的正确率,否则会造成读而无解,还不如不读。

四、浏览式阅读

在练习速读的过程中,可采用浏览式阅读的方式。如看报时,练习眼睛的快速移动,还可复读一些内容已经非常熟悉、语言相对较简单、易读易懂的文章、小说,甚至阅读一些浅显易懂的母语材料。其实,速读的习惯是长期养成的。

五、网上泛读

网上泛读指的是通过互联网进行泛读,这是目前最为便捷的阅读方式之一。通过滚动字幕的阅读自然可以控制阅读速度,还可以避免回读,这种方式也能有效提高阅读的速度。

第四节　英语阅读中应处理好的几个关系

一、对待阅读的不同态度

不同的文化或国度持不同的读书态度。一位叫梁厚甫[美]的网友在《美国人的读书态度》(2008)一文中认为,中国人受传统观念"万般皆下品,唯有读书高"的影响,到现在依然对读书的观念过于正式和隆重。有一点钱的人家,都有一间专为读书而设的书房,较次的,也会在自己的卧室里设一张书桌,书大多放在书房的书柜里,所以读书就应到书房正坐而读。而美国人视读书为一件平常已极的事情,其平常有如搔头和抓耳朵一般。大多数西方人没有书房,书到处都是,客厅、厨房、洗手间、洗漱间、卧室、阁楼里,却能随时随地读书,就连蹲厕所也会翻翻书或杂志。中国把读书人视为一种特殊的人物,因此,读书也变成一种神秘的事情。美国人的读书态度之所以可取,就是因为美国人把读书视为生活的一部分。对读书的结果不要期望过高。正确的读书态度是有空便要读书,不读书,浪费光阴,未免可惜。中国学生中,如果别人在打牌或游戏,有人在旁边看书,可能会遭到嘲笑,或者自己跑到外面去看书。

有一些人舍不得花钱买书,就连教材都不想买,然而过生日却搞得十分隆重。现在,很少有人送礼时送书。买书者或为真正要读,或为装饰之用。前者买的是实用的,后者大多买的是大部头的精装本。

西方人随身总要带上一本书,有空就读;而中国人随身听MP3或MP4,听音乐者较多。中国人仍然把读书看得太正式,只有在书桌旁、阅览室才能读书。有的大学生甚至上课时都不带书,更谈不上业余时间看书学习了。正确的做法是把读书看成跟吃饭一样,是生活中不可或缺的重要部分之一,从而养成读书的习惯。

二、精读与泛读

弗朗西施·培根说过:"有些书可浅尝,有些书需生吞,仅少数书须嚼烂消化。"古人云:读书千遍,心到、眼到、口到(指朗读)。

精泛各异、精泛结合。"精"要精到意—构—格—形—颂—忆—辨:意——文章之意(主旨和词义——本义与引申);构——结构,表现形式与手法;格——风格;形——形式;颂——诵读,上口,随手随口就来;忆——记忆,把知识变为自己的一部分;辨——辨别,批判性的吸收与评判。①

"泛"是内容广泛,包括所感兴趣者、所需应用者、所关联者;"泛"又为概要性的了解,把握中心思想、主旨即可。

精泛结合,精中有泛,泛中有精,泛为精之先行,精为泛之深入。

古人曰:"读书破万卷,下笔如有神。""破"乃"剖析"之意,就是说要把书读懂、读透。只有读懂了、读透了,又读得"博"了,这样才会"下笔如有神"。

三、无声阅读与有声阅读

阅读也可分为朗读(Vocal Reading)和默读(Non-vocal Reading)。为了掌握外语学习的"听、说、读、写"四会的能力,学习者必须要正确运用有声阅读与无声阅读。听说和口译需要有声阅读,而阅读、写作和笔译则需要无声阅读。因为只有默读才能提高阅读速度。朗读的速度非常有限,无法达到快速阅读的要求——每分钟数百字到数千字。美国斯坦福大学教育学博士林恩·布德罗斯(Dr. Lynn Boudreux)要求他的助手杨每天至少要阅读数十万甚至上百万字的资料。然而对于学习外语来说,朗读也是非常重要的技能。它是训练听力和说的能力的重要途径。每天要坚持大声朗读 20—30 分钟。朗读时要注意发音准确、语调正确、意群停顿正确,要流利地传达出文本的意思。听力训练也不可少,每天坚持 1 小时左右。它是为朗读提供模仿的标准的音调、语流。朗读

---

① 周荣辉. 英语阅读理解策略与技巧[M]. 成都:西南交通大学出版社,2009.

第五章　英语阅读教学中的方法掌握探索

和默读不是截然分开的,在实际的学习中,二者又是互补的。在默读中,遇到经典语句也可大声诵读;在朗读之前,也可以对材料事先浏览一遍,知其大意后再行朗读会达到绘声绘色的效果。

四、自下而上阅读、自上而下阅读和交互阅读模式

这三种阅读模式绝不是孤立的,相反,它们是相辅相成的且互补性很强。在学习过程中,具体使用哪种模式要根据阅读目的、文体、容许的时间而定。特别要注意的是,阅读模式与按文章或书籍的编排顺序是有区别的。一般来说,自上而下就是指从头到尾的阅读模式;自下而上就是先读文章或书籍的末尾章节或段落,有需要回答问题的文章,先看问题再读文章的阅读模式。这是两个完全不同的概念,不可混为一谈。

第六章 英语阅读教学经典研读实践探索

上述各章节主要研究了英语阅读与教学的相关理论知识,本章基于教学实践,结合经典阅读案例展开分析,帮助学习者深入把握英语阅读技巧,提升自身的阅读能力。

第一节 示范性阅读与解析

一、示范性阅读语篇

Passage 1

The Story of a Beggar and a Ring

This was a very honest beggar.

One day, he knocked at the door of a luxurious mansion. The butler came out and said, "Yes, sir? What do you wish, my good man?"

The beggar answered, "Just a bit of charity, for the love of God."

"I shall have to take this up with the lady of the house."

The butler consulted with the lady of the house and she, who was very miserly, answered, "Jeremiah, give that good man a loaf of bread. One only. And, if possible, one from yesterday."

Jeremiah, who was secretly in love with his employer, sought out a stale loaf of bread, hard as a rock, and handed it to the beggar.

"Here you are, my good man," he said, no longer calling him "sir".

"God bless you," the beggar answered.

Jeremiah closed the massive oaken door, and the beggar went off with the loaf of bread under his arm. He came to the vacant lot where he spent his days and nights. He sat down in the shade of a tree, and began to eat the bread. Suddenly he bit into a hard object and felt one of his molars crumble to pieces. Great was his surprise when he picked up, together with the fragments of his molar, a fine ring of gold, pearls and diamonds.

"What luck," he said to himself, "I'll sell it and I'll have money for a long time."

But his honesty immediately prevailed. "No," he added, "I'll seek out its owner and return it."

Inside the ring were engraved the initials J. X. Neither unintelligent nor lazy, the beggar went to a store and asked for the telephone book. He found that, in the entire town, there existed only one family whose surname began with X: the Xofaina family.

Filled with joy for being able to put his honesty into practice, he set out for the home of the Xofaina family. Great was his amazement when he saw it was the very house at which he had been given the loaf of bread containing the ring. He knocked at the door.

Jeremiah emerged and asked him, "What do you wish, my good man?"

The beggar answered, "I've found this ring inside the loaf of bread you were good enough to give me a while ago."

Jeremiah took the ring and said, "I shall have to take this up with the lady of the house."

He consulted with the lady of the house, and she, happy and fairly singing, exclaimed, "Lucky me! Here we are with the ring I had lost last week, while I was kneading the dough for the bread! These are my initials, J. X., which stand for my name: Josermina Xofaina."

After a moment of reflection, she added, "Jeremiah, go and give that good man whatever he wants as a reward. As long as it's not very expensive."

Jeremiah returned to the door and said to the beggar, "My good man, tell me what you would like as a reward for you kind act."

The beggar answered, "Just a loaf of bread to satisfy my hunger."

Jeremiah, who was still in love with his employer, sought out an old loaf of bread, hard as a rock, and handed it to the beggar.

"Here you are, my good man."

"God bless you."

Jeremiah shut the massive oaken door, and the beggar went off with the loaf of bread under his arm. He came to the vacant lot in which he spent his days and nights. He sat down in the shade of a tree and began to eat the bread. Suddenly, he bit into a hard object and felt another of his molars crumble to pieces. Great was his surprise when he picked up, along with the fragments of his second broken molar, another fine ring of gold, pearls and diamonds.

Once more he noticed the initials J. X. Once more he returned the ring to Josermina Xofaina and as a reward received a third loaf of hard bread, in which he found a third ring that he again returned, and for which he obtained, as a reward, a fourth loaf of hard bread, in which…

From that fortunate day until the unlucky day of his death, the beggar lived happily and without financial problems. He only had to return the ring he found inside the bread every day.

判断对错：

1. The beggar came to a very rich lady's house to beg.

2. The house owner was a very generous lady.

3. She asked her butler to give the beggar a loaf of stale bread.

4. The butler was secretly in love with her.

5. The beggar wanted to sell the ring at first when he found it in the bread.

6. He was so honest that he returned the ring to the owner, the lady of the house.

7. The lady was so grateful this time that she became very generous to the beggar.

8. The butler gave the beggar another loaf of hard bread.

9. Each time, the beggar was satisfied with the stale bread given by the butler.

10. The beggar earned his living by being honest.

Passage 2

John Roebling's Story

In 1868, a creative engineer named John Roebling was inspired by an idea to build a spectacular bridge connecting New York with the Long Island. However, bridge-building experts throughout the world thought that this was an impossible feat and told Roebling to forget the idea. It just could not be done. It was not practical. It had never been done before.

However, Roebling could not ignore the vision he had in his mind of this bridge. He thought about it all the time and he knew deep in his heart that it could be done. He just had to share the dream with someone else. After much discussion and persuasion, he managed to convince his son, Washington Roebling, an up-and-coming engineer, that the bridge in fact could be built.

Working together for the first time, the father and the son developed concepts of how it could be accomplished and how the obstacles could be overcome. With great excitement and inspiration, and a wild challenge before them, they hired their crew and began to build their dream bridge.

The project started well, but when it was only a few months underway, a tragic accident on the site took the life of John Roebling. Washington was injured and left with a certain amount of brain damage, which resulted in him not being able to walk, talk or even move.

"We told them so."

"Crazy men and their crazy dreams."

"It's foolish to chase wild visions."

Everyone had a negative comment to make and felt that the project should be scrapped since the Roeblings were the only ones who knew how the bridge could be built. In spite of his handicap, Washington was never discouraged and still had a burning desire to complete the bridge. His mind was still as sharp as ever.

He tried to inspire and pass on his enthusiasm to some of his friends, but they were too discouraged by the task. As he lay on his bed in his hospital room, with the sunlight streaming through the windows, a gentle breeze blew the thin white curtains apart and he was able to see the sky and the tops of the trees outside for just a moment.

It seemed that there was a message for him not to give up. Suddenly, an idea hit him. All he could do was move one finger and he decided to make the best use of it. By moving this finger, he slowly developed a code of communication with his wife.

He touched his wife's arm with that finger, indicating to her that he wanted her to call the engineers again. Then he used the same method of tapping her arm to tell the engineers what to do. It seemed foolish, but the project was underway again.

For 13 years, Washington tapped out his instructions with his finger on his wife's arm, until the bridge was finally completed. Today, the spectacular Brooklyn Bridge stands in all its glory as a tribute to the triumph of one man's never-say-die spirit and his determination not to be defeated by circumstances. It is also a tribute to the engineers and their teamwork, and to their faith in a man who was considered mad by half the world. It stands too as a tangible monument to the love and devotion of his wife, who, for 13 long years, patiently decoded the messages of her husband and told the engineers what to do.

Perhaps this is one of the best examples of a never-say-die attitude that overcomes a terrible physical handicap and achieves an impossible goal.

判断对错：

1. John Roebling's idea of building a bridge connecting New York with the Long Island was welcomed by bridge experts all over the world.

2. Roebling didn't lose heart even though others considered it an impossible dream.

3. Roebling succeeded in winning the support from his son after much discussion and persuasion.

4. The father and the son had cooperated before the construction of the Brooklyn Bridge.

5. The tragic accident shortly after the start of the construction

killed the father and seriously injured the son.

6. The whole world responded to the accident by feeling sympathetic and making encouraging comments.

7. Washington, though unable to speak after the accident, was able to think clearly and logically.

8. Washington talked to his wife, who passed the instructions on to the other engineers.

9. The construction of the bridge is a tribute to Washington's determination, to the confidence of his workers and to the love and devotion of his wife.

10. The story aims to tell us that where there is a will, there is a way.

二、阅读语篇译文与解析

Passage 1

参考译文：

乞丐和戒指的故事

他是一个非常诚实的乞丐。

有一天,他敲了一座豪宅的门。管家出来说道:"哎,阁下。你想要什么,我的先生?"

乞丐答道:"看在热爱上帝的份上,行行好吧!"

"这事儿我得告诉女主人。"

管家问了女主人。这位女主人十分吝啬。她说:"杰拉米,给那个先生一个面包吧。只给一个。对了,如果有,给他昨天的。"

杰拉米暗恋着他的主人,为了讨好她,从家里找出一个硬得像石头一样的面包,递给了乞丐。

"拿着吧,我的先生。"他说,不再叫他"阁下"了。

"上帝保佑你。"乞丐回答。

杰拉米关上了橡木大门,乞丐掖着面包离开了。他来到了他度日过夜的那块空地,坐在树荫下,开始吃面包。突然,他咬到了一个硬邦邦的东西,觉得一个牙齿已经破碎了。使他吃惊的是,他捡起他的碎牙时,发现了一枚由黄金、珍珠和钻石做成的戒指。

"多好的运气啊,"他自言自语地说,"我要卖了它,很长时间就不会缺钱用了。"

但是,他的诚实立即占了上风。"不,"他接着说,"我要找到它的主人,把这东西交还给他。"

戒指的里圈刻着缩写字母 J. X. 。乞丐既不傻,也不懒,他走到一家商店,要了电话号码簿。他发现,全镇只有 Xofaina 这一户人家的姓是以 X 开头的。

他怀着能将诚实付诸实践的高兴心情。开始寻找 Xofaina 一家的住所。使他十分惊讶的是,他发现那竟然是给他内含戒指的面包的那户人家。他敲了敲门。

杰拉米出来问他:"你想要什么,我的先生?"

乞丐回答:"我在你刚才给我的面包里面发现了这个戒指。"

杰拉米接过戒指说:"这件事我得告诉女主人。"

他问了女主人,女主人高兴地唱了起来。她大声说道:"我真幸运啊!上星期我和面的时候丢失了这枚戒指,现在又回来了。J. X. 是我名字 Josermina Xofaina 的缩写。"

沉思片刻后,她接着说:"杰拉米,去拿个东西谢谢那个先生吧,他要什么就给什么,只要不太贵就行。"

杰拉米回到门口,对乞丐说:"我的先生,告诉我,你想要得到什么东西来报答你的善举。"

乞丐回答:"给一个面包充饥就行了。"

杰拉米依然爱着他的雇主,为了讨好她,从家里又找出了一个硬得如石头般的面包,递给了乞丐。

"拿着吧,我的先生。"

"上帝保佑你。"

杰拉米关上了橡木大门,乞丐掖着面包离开了。他来到了他度日过夜的那块空地,坐在树荫下,开始吃面包。突然,他咬到了一个硬邦邦的东西,觉得又一个牙齿破碎了。使他吃惊的是,当他捡起他的第二颗碎牙时,又发现了一枚由黄金、珍珠和钻石做成的戒指。

他又一次看到了缩写字母 J. X.,也又一次把戒指退还给 Josermina Xofaina。并得到了作为酬谢的第三只面包,在里面发现了第三枚戒指,又把这枚戒指退还。作为酬谢,又得到第四只面包,在里面……

从那个幸运之日开始,直到他不幸去世,这个乞丐都过着幸福的、不再没有钱的生活。他每天只需要做一件事。那就是归还面包里的戒指。
答案及解析:
1. T 2. F 3. T 4. T 5. T 6. T 7. F 8. T 9. T 10. T

Passage 2
参考译文:

约翰·罗勃林的故事

1868年,一位名叫约翰·罗勃林的极富创造力的工程师,想到了一个主意,要建造一座连接纽约和长岛的大桥。然而,全世界的桥梁专家都觉得这么庞大的工程是不可能实现的,要罗勃林别再痴心妄想了。这根本就是不可行,不实际,这样的事情以前从来没有人做过。

罗勃林无法忘却脑海中已经形成的大桥形象。他每时每刻都在想着这座桥,并且在内心深处知道这是可以完成的。他必须和其他人谈谈自己的这个梦想。经过多次讨论和劝说,他终于使他的儿子华盛顿——一名年轻有为的工程师——相信这座桥事实上是可以建成的。

父子俩初次合作,对如何建成这座桥以及如何克服各种困难想出了各种对策。面对着如此巨大的挑战,他们既激动又振奋,便雇人开始建造他们的梦中之桥。

一开始工程很顺利,但是刚过几个月,工地上就发生了惨祸,夺走了罗勃林的生命,华盛顿也受了重伤,脑部受到一定损伤。他无法走路,不能说话,甚至无法动弹。

"我们告诉过他们,这是不行的。"

"只有疯子才有这样疯狂的想法。"

"追逐疯狂的梦想,真是太傻了。"

所有人都在批评他们,觉得这项工程应该取消,因为罗勃林父子是仅有的知道如何建造这座桥的人。然而,华盛顿尽管是身残之人,但从没灰心过。他仍然急切地想要建成这座桥,他的思维和以前一样敏捷。

他竭力让他的一些朋友振作起来,也想以自己对工程的激情感染他们,但是他们被这个工程吓倒了。他躺在医院的病床上,阳光从窗外泻入,微风吹开了薄纱窗帘,那一刻他看到了外面的天空以及高高的树冠。

这好像是在向他传递一个信息,让他永远不要放弃。突然间,他有了主意。他唯一能做的是移动一个手指。于是,他决定充分利用这个手指。通过摆动这个手指,他慢慢地研究出一种和妻子交流的方法。

他用这个手指触碰妻子的手臂,示意他想让她再把工程师们召集起来。然后他用同样的办法,轻碰他妻子的手臂,让她告诉那些工程师该做些什么。这个方法看起来很傻,但是工程又启动了。

华盛顿用他的手指在他妻子手臂上敲出了种种指示,13年后,大桥终于落成。如今,布罗克林大桥巍然屹立,这是对他不屈不挠的精神和不为困境击败的坚强意志取得胜利的敬意;它也是对造桥工程师及其团队的敬意,在那么多人认为罗勃林是疯子的时候,他们对他却深信不疑。它还是一座伸手可及的丰碑,纪念他妻子的关爱和奉献。在漫长的13年里,她耐心地破译着来自丈夫手指的信息并给工程师们下达任务。

这也许是永不言败的最佳事例之一,这种精神克服了可怕的生理残疾,实现了异常艰难的目标。

答案及解析:

1. F 2. T 3. T 4. F 5. T
6. F 7. T 8. F 9. T 10. T

第二节 经典美文阅读与解析

一、诗歌阅读

(一)《一朵红红的玫瑰》

原文:

A Red, Red Rose

Robert Burns

O, my Luve's like a red, red rose,

That's newly sprung in June;

O, my Luve's like the melodie,

第六章　英语阅读教学经典研读实践探索

That's sweetly play'd in tune.

As fair art thou, my bonnie lass,
So deep in luve am I,
And I will luve thee still, my Dear,
Till a' the seas gang dry.

Till a' the seas gang dry, my Dear,
And the rocks melt wi' the sun!
And I will luve thee still, my Dear,
While the sands o' life shall run.

And fare thee weel, my only Luve,
And fare thee weel, a while!
And I will come again, my Luve,
Tho' it were ten thousand mile!

译文：

一朵红红的玫瑰

呵，我的爱人像朵红红的玫瑰，
六月里迎风初开；
呵，我的爱人像支甜甜的曲子，
奏得合拍又和谐。

我的好姑娘，多么美丽的人儿！
请看我，多么深挚的爱情！
亲爱的，我永远爱你，
纵使大海干涸水流尽。

纵使大海干涸水流尽，
太阳将岩石烧作灰尘，
亲爱的，我永远爱你，
只要我一息犹存。

珍重吧，我唯一的爱人，
珍重吧，让我们暂时别离，
但我定要回来，
哪怕千里万里！

(王佐良 译)

作者简介及作品欣赏：

  罗伯特·彭斯(Robert Burns,1759—1796)是苏格兰著名的农民诗人。他生于贫苦的农民家庭，只读过两年书。自幼受其父熏陶喜爱诗歌。彭斯一生清贫，大半生劳作于田间，因此他的作品能真实地反映出苏格兰农民的思想和渴望。1786年，他的第一部诗集《苏格兰方言诗集》(Poems,Chiefly in the Scottish Dialect,1786)一出版，就受到了农民的热烈欢迎，也引起了文学界和社会人士的广泛注意。他的诗歌创作具有民主进步的思想。这方面的代表作有《自由树》(The Tree of Liberty)和《苏格兰人》(Scots Wha Hae)。在这两首诗中，诗人歌颂了法国大革命，号召苏格兰人民起来反抗英国压迫者。《两只狗》(The Two Dogs)和《威力长老的祈祷》(Holy Willie's Prayer)是对地主阶级的荒淫无耻、教会的虚伪的尖锐讽刺。彭斯还创作了大量抒情诗来歌颂自然的壮美、劳动人民的淳朴以及友谊和爱情，如《我的心呀在高原》(My Heart's in the Highlands)、《一朵红红的玫瑰》(A Red,Red Rose)、《约翰·安德生，我的爱人》(John Anderson,My Jo)等。彭斯对苏格兰民歌的整理、传播和发展作出了突出的贡献。他把诗与民歌紧紧结合起来，一生编写了歌谣360多篇，其中100多篇传播至今。《友谊地久天长》(Auld Lang Syne)已成为世界人民传唱的佳作。彭斯的诗主旨鲜明，淳朴自然，富有乡土气息。诗句通俗流畅，便于吟唱，在民间广为流传。

  《一朵红红的玫瑰》是彭斯留给世人的一份宝贵的文化遗产和精神财富。诗歌语言纯朴却不失生动，简短却饱含深情，虽没有深刻的寓意但温馨无比，让人充分领略到爱情的动人与美丽。诗人用流畅悦耳的音调、质朴无华的词语和热烈真挚的情感打动了千百万恋人的心，使得这首诗在问世之后成为人们传唱不衰的经典。全诗无论意象、结构、修辞还是遣词造句都自然优美，浑然天成，清新质朴的民歌诗体又使其乐感倍增，给人以极大的美的享受。

(二)《未选择的路》

原文：

The Road Not Taken

Robert Frost

Two roads diverged in a yellow wood,
And sorry I could not travel both
And be one traveler, long I stood
And looked down one as far as I could
To where it bent in the undergrowth;

Then took the other, as just as fair,
And having perhaps the better claim,
Because it was grassy and wanted wear;
Though as for that the passing there
Had worn them really about the same,

And both that morning equally lay
In leaves no step had trodden black.
Oh, I kept the first for another day!
Yet knowing how way leads on to way,
I doubted if I should ever come back.

I shall be telling this with a sigh
Somewhere ages and ages hence:
Two roads diverged in a wood, and I—
I took the one less traveled by,
And that has made all the difference.

译文：

未选择的路

黄色的树林里分出两条路，
可惜我不能同时去涉足，
我在那路口久久伫立，
我向着一条路极目望去，
直到它消失在丛林深处。

但我却选了另外一条路，
它荒草萋萋，十分幽寂，
显得更诱人，更美丽；
虽然在这两条小路上，
都很少留下旅人的足迹；

虽然那天清晨落叶满地，
两条路都未经脚印污染。
呵，留下一条路等改日再见！
但我知道路径延绵无尽头，
恐怕我难以再回返。

也许多少年后在某个地方，
我将轻声叹息将往事回顾：
一片树林里分出两条路——
而我选了人迹更少的一条
从此决定了我一生的道路。

(顾子欣 译)

作者简介及作品欣赏：

罗伯特·弗洛斯特(Robert Frost, 1874—1963)，美国现代著名诗人。出生于旧金山，10岁迁居新英格兰，求学于哈佛大学，两年后缀学。他当过农民、工人和教师。他喜爱农村，常描写农村风光，素有"农民诗人"之称。后来，他当过大学教授、驻校诗人和国会图书馆诗学顾问，有美国非官方的"桂冠诗人"之称，先后4次获美国"普利策文学奖"，被誉为美国的"民族诗人"。他的诗歌大多采用传统的格律形式，用语浅近而造意隽永，内容主要以新英格兰农村为背景，描写自然景色和朴实的田园生活，这对于受工业化、城市化等弊端困扰的美国人来说，更具有吸引力。

弗洛斯特 19 岁时就公开发表了他的第一首诗，但长期默默无闻，直到他 39 岁时，第一部诗集《少年的心愿》(A Boy's Will, 1912)在英国伦敦问世，他的诗歌创作生涯才算正式开始。两年后《波士顿以北》(North of Boston, 1914)的出版使他蜚声诗坛。此后，他的诗篇接踵而来，名震大西洋两岸。他的主要诗集有：《山间》(Mountain Interval, 1916)、《新罕布什尔》(New Hampshire, 1923)、《诗集》(Collected Poems, 1930)、《见证树》(A Witness Tree, 1942)、《诗歌全集》(Complete Poems, 1949)、《林中空地》(In the Clearing, 1962)等。

他的诗歌在形式上与传统诗歌相近，但不像浪漫派、唯美派诗人那样矫揉造作。他的诗往往以描写新英格兰的自然景色或风土人情开始，渐渐进入哲理的境界。他的诗朴实无华，然而细致含蓄，耐人回味。著名的诗篇《补墙》(Mending Wall, 1914)写人世间存在着许多有形与无形的墙；《白桦树》(Birches, 1916)写人总想逃避现实，但终究要回到现实中来；《火与冰》(Fire and Ice)意在说明人与人之间的冷漠关系足以毁灭人类社会。

《未选择的路》是弗洛斯特的著名诗篇。它通过对林间择路这样一件小事的具体描述，表达了一个抽象而又深邃的人生哲理：人一生中的机遇有限，一个人一辈子只能从事于一种职业，居于一个家庭，过着一种生活；人生道路上的选择既有自由意志，又受种种限制与影响。诗中，诗人回忆一次林间择路的往事，他伫立路口，难以抉择，只见其中一条的尽头消失在灌木树丛。考虑再三，他选择了另一条，因为那条路上杂草丛生，无人行走。但他走过以后，此路漫布足迹，跟那一条并无区别。他走过这条路以后，常希望有朝一日能再走另外那一条。但是人生的道路是难以返回的。此诗是作者对自己选择了诗人这条道路的回顾与反思。全诗 4 节，5 行体，韵脚均为 ABAAB，工整平稳。

二、散文阅读

(一)《论读书》

原文:

Of Studies

Francis Bacon

Studies serve for delight, for ornament, and for ability. Their chief use for delight, is in privateness and retiring; for ornament, is in discourse; and for ability, is in the judgment and disposition of business. For expert men can execute, and perhaps judge of particulars, one by one; but the general counsels, and the plots and marshalling of affairs come best from those that are learned. To spend too much time in studies is sloth; to use them too much for ornament is affectation; to make judgment wholly by their rules is the humor of a scholar. They perfect nature, and are perfected by experience: for natural abilities are like natural plants that need pruning by study; and studies themselves do give forth directions too much at large, except they be bounded in by experience. Crafty men contemn studies, simple men admire them, and wise men use them; for they teach not their own use; but that is a wisdom without them, and above them, won by observation. Read not to contradict and confute, nor to believe and take for granted, nor to find talk and discourse, but to weigh and consider. Some books are to be tasted, others to be swallowed, and some few to be chewed and digested: that is, some books are to be read only in parts; others to be read, but not curiously; and some few to be read wholly, and with diligence and attention. Some books also may be read by deputy, and extracts made of them by others; but that would be only in the less important arguments and the meaner sort of books; else distilled books are like common distilled waters, flashy things.

Reading makes a full man, conference a ready man, and writing an exact man. And, therefore, if a man write little, he had need have a great memory; if he confer little, he had need have a present wit; and if he read little, he had need have much cunning to seem to know that he doth not. Histories make men wise, poets witty, the mathematics subtle, natural philosophy deep, moral grave, logic and rhetoric able to contend. Abeunt studia in mores. Nay, there is no stond or impediment in the wit but may be wrought out by fit studies; like as diseases of the body may have appropriate exercises. Bowling is good for the stone and reins, shooting for the lungs and breast, gentle walking for the stomach, riding for the head, and the like. So if a man's wit be wandering, let him study the mathematics, for in demonstrations, if his wit be called away never so little, he must begin again. If his wit be not apt to distinguish or find differences, let him study the schoolmen, for they are cymini sectors. If he be not apt to beat over matters and to call up one thing to prove and illustrate another, let him study the lawyers' cases. So every defect of the mind may have a special receipt.

译文：

论读书

读书足以怡情，足以博彩，足以长才。其怡情也，最见于独处幽居之时；其博彩也，最见于高谈阔论之中；其长才也，最见于处世判事之际。练达之士虽能分别处理细事或一一判别枝节，然纵观统筹，全局策划，则舍好学深思者莫属。读书费时过多易惰，文采藻饰太盛则矫，全凭条文断事乃学究故态。读书补天然不足，经验又补读书之不足，盖天生才干犹如自然花草，读书然后知如何修剪移接；而书中所示，如不以经验范之，则又大而无当。有一技之长者鄙读书，无知者羡读书，唯明智之士用读书，然书并不以用处告人，用书之智不在书中，而在书外，全凭观察得之。读书时不可存心诘难作者，不可尽信书上所言，亦不可只为寻章摘句，而应推敲细思。书有浅尝者，有可吞食者，少数则须咀嚼消化。换言之，有只须读其部分者，有只须大体涉猎者，少数则须全读，读时须全神贯注，孜孜不倦。书亦可请人代读，取其所作摘要，但只限题材较次或价值不高者，否则书经提炼犹如水经蒸馏，淡而无味矣。

读书使人充实，讨论使人机智，笔记使人准确。因此不常作笔记者须记忆特强，不常讨论者须天生聪颖，不常读书者须欺世有术，始能无知而显有知。读史使人明智，读诗使人灵秀，数学使人周密，科学使人深刻，伦理使人庄重，逻辑修辞之学使人善辩；凡有所学，皆成性格。人之才智但有滞碍，无不可读适当之书使之顺畅，一如身体百病，皆可借适宜之运动除之。滚球利睾肾，射箭利胸肺，慢步宜肠胃，骑术利头脑，诸如此类。如智力不集中，可令读数学，盖演题须全神贯注，稍有分散即须重演；如不能辨异，可令读经院哲学，盖是辈皆吹毛求疵之人；如不善求同，不善以一物阐证另一物，可令读律师之案卷。如此头脑中凡有缺陷，皆有特药可医。

作者简介及作品欣赏：

弗朗西斯·培根(Francis Bacon, 1561—1626)是英国文艺复兴时期著名的哲学家、政治家和散文家，1561年1月22日出生于伦敦一个贵族家庭。早年进入剑桥大学三一学院(Trinity College)学习自然科学，后又学习法律，曾作过检察总长和大法官。1618年任大理院院长，封为勋爵。1621年因受贿被弹劾去职，嗣后家居著述。他致力于科学实验和写作。他在科学方面的主要贡献在于他的科学实验思想和关于自然科学研究的分类思考方法。培根关于科学方面的主要著作全部是用拉丁文写成的。1626年冬，培根在野外试验雪的防腐作用时受寒致死。

培根的主要建树在哲学方面。他自称"以天下全部学问为己任"，企图"将全部科学、技术和人类的一切知识全面重建"，并为此计划写一部大书，总名《伟大的复兴》(The Great Instauration)，虽然只完成两部分，但已产生重大影响。他强调通过实验去揭示自然界的秘密，获取知识，并认为"知识就是力量"。主要作品有《学术的进步》(Advancement of Learning, 1605)、《新工具》(Novum Organum, 1620)、《新大西岛》(The New Atlantis, 1626)。

培根对社会、生活、人生有着敏锐的观察力，并对道德观念、政治体制、宗教信仰、社会生活等方面作出了冷静的观察及充满智慧与哲理的评论，写就了许多关于社会生活和人生哲理的散文。他的散文形式庄重，句法严谨，文笔紧凑、锐利；他对每个题目都有独到之见，说理透彻，警句迭出，很富诗意。英国本无随笔，由于培根的示范，随笔才在英国扎根，后来写随笔的名家辈出，随笔也成为英国文学中有特色的体裁之一，对此培根有开创之功。

第六章　英语阅读教学经典研读实践探索

《随笔》(*Essays*)是培根在文学方面的主要著作,初版于 1597 年,只收集 10 篇极短的摘记式文章;经 1612 年、1625 年两次增补扩充,才收入短文 58 篇,然而它在英国文学史上却占有重要的地位。《随笔》的内容涉及哲学思想、伦理探讨、为官秘诀、处事之道、治家准则及对艺术和大自然的欣赏等。

在《论读书》(*Of Studies*)中,培根用极简练的语言分析了读书的目的及读书的益处。他认为不同的人是带着不同的目的、持不同的态度去读书的,并提出了读书的正确方法,反对读死书和死读书,提倡学以致用,用实践检验书本知识的效用。

(二)《怎样步入老年》

原文:

How to Grow Old
Bertrand Russell

Psychologically there are two dangers to be guarded against in old age. One of these is undue absorption in the past. It does not do to live in memories, in regrets for the good old days, or in sadness about friends who are dead. One's thoughts must be directed to the future, and to things about which there is something to be done. This is not always easy: one's own past is a gradually increasing weight. It is easy to think to oneself that one's emotions used to be more vivid than they are, and one's mind more keen. If this is true it should be forgotten, and if it is forgotten it will probably not be true.

The other thing to be avoided is clinging to youth in the hope of sucking vigor from its vitality. When your children are grown up they want to live their own lives, and if you continue to be as interested in them as you were when they were young, you are likely to become a burden to them, unless they are unusually callous. I do not mean that one should be without interest in them, but one's interest should be contemplative and, if possible, philanthropic, but not unduly emotional. Animals become indifferent to their young as soon as their young can look after themselves, but human beings, owing to the length of infancy, find this difficult.

I think that a successful old age is easiest for those who have strong impersonal interests involving appropriate activities. It is in this sphere that long experience is really fruitful, and it is in this sphere that the wisdom born of experience can be exercised without being oppressive. It is no use telling grown-up children not to make mistakes, both because they will not believe you, and because mistakes are an essential part of education. But if you are one of those who are incapable of impersonal interests, you may find that your life will be empty unless you concern yourself with your children and grandchildren. In that case you must realize that while you can still render them material services, such as making them an allowance or knitting them jumpers, you must not expect that they will enjoy your company.

Some old people are oppressed by the fear of death. In the young there is a justification for this feeling. Young men who have reason to fear that they will be killed in battle may justifiably feel bitter in the thought that they have been cheated of the best things that life has to offer. But in an old man who has known human joys and sorrows, and has achieved whatever work it was in him to do, the fear of death is somewhat abject and ignoble. The best way to overcome it—so at least it seems to me—is to make your interests gradually wider and more impersonal, until bit by bit the walls of the ego recede, and your life becomes increasingly merged in the universal life. An individual human existence should be like a river—small at first, narrowly contained within its banks, and rushing passionately past boulders and over waterfalls. Gradually the river grows wider, the banks recede, the waters flow more quietly, and in the end, without any visible break, they become merged in the sea, and painlessly lose their individual being. The man who, in old age, can see his life in this way, will not suffer from the fear of death, since the things he cares for will continue. And if, with the decay of vitality, weariness increases, the thought of rest will not be unwelcome. I should wish to die while still at work, knowing that others will carry on what I can no longer do, and content in the thought that what was possible has been done.

译文：
怎样步入老年

　　从心理学上来讲，在老年时期要防止这样两种危险：第一是过分沉湎于过去。生活在过去之中，为流逝的好时光而后悔，或因朋友作古而痛苦，这些都是没有什么用处的。人的思想应该朝着未来，朝着还可以有所作为的方面。这并不是容易做到的，因为一个人的过去是一份不断加重的负担。人们容易承认自己过去的感情，比现在丰富；自己过去的思想，比现在深刻。如果这是事实，就把它忘掉。如果忘掉它，那它就不可能成为事实。

　　另外一件要避免的事情是依附于年轻人，渴望从他们的活力中汲取力量。当你的孩子们已经长大，他们就要过属于他们自己的生活，如果你还是像小时候那样对他们关心备至，你就可能成为他们的负担，除非他们对此毫无知觉。我并不是说应该对他们不闻不问，但是你所给予的关心应是理性的、慷慨的（如果可能的话），而非过于感情用事。动物在自己的后代一旦能够生活自理时，就不再给予照顾，可是人类，因为幼年时期太长，很难做到这一点。

　　我觉得一个人能做到对合适的活动兴趣盎然、不理会自己的个人得失，那么，他就很容易享有成功的晚年，因为经过长期积累的经验在此可以结出累累的硕果，而通过经验产生的智慧在这个时候既有用武之地，而又不至咄咄逼人。让已经长大成人的孩子不要犯错误是没有好处的，因为他们不会信任你，同时也由于犯错误是接受教育的不可缺少的一环。但如果你做不到不计个人得失，那么，不将你的心放在儿孙后辈身上，你便会觉得生活空虚无聊。如果是这样，你必须知道：尽管你还能给他们物质上的帮助，诸如给点补贴或织几件毛衣，可是你千万不要指望他们会喜欢跟你在一起。

　　有些老人被死亡的恐惧所困扰。假如年轻人有这种恐惧，那是没有什么可说的。年轻人有理由害怕战死在战场上；但当他们想到被骗走了生命所能赋予的美好生活时，他们有理由表示不满。但对于一个尝尽人间疾苦，已经完成该做的一切的老年人来讲，怕死就有点不大好了。克服这种恐惧的最好办法是——至少在我看来是这样的——使你的爱好逐渐扩大，越来越超出个人的范围，最后你的自我之墙将一点一点地退却,你的生命将越来越和人类的生命融合在一起。一个人的一生应该像一条河——开始水流很小,被两岸紧紧地束缚着,激烈地冲过岩石和瀑布。渐渐地它变宽了,两岸退却了,河水静静地流着。到最后,不经过任何可见的停留,就和大海汇合在一起,毫无痛苦地失去它自身的存在。一个在老年能这样对待生活的人,将不会感到死亡的恐惧,因为他所关心的事物将继续下去。假如由于生命力的减退,倦意日增,安息的想法也许就是可喜之处。我希望我能死于工作之时,并且在我快死的时候能知道别人将继续做我不能再做的工作,同时能为自己已完成力所能及的一切而心满意足。

作者简介及作品欣赏:

伯特兰·罗素(Bertrand Russell,1872—1970)英国哲学家、数学家和逻辑学家。出生于英国贵族家庭。早在 11 岁时就对宗教产生怀疑,这种情况决定了罗素哲学生涯的风格和目标,使得他成为 20 世纪声誉卓著、影响深远的思想家之一。1950 年获诺贝尔文学奖。20 世纪 50 年代以后,他的注意力从哲学转移到国际政治方面,是世界和平运动的倡导者。1954 年,他在英国 BBC 广播电台发表了著名的广播讲演《人类的险境》(*Man's Peril*)以谴责氢弹实验,随后又发表了《罗素—爱因斯坦声明》(*Russell-Einstein Manifesto*)。1958 年发起禁止核武器的示威运动。19 世纪 60 年代后期,他猛烈攻击美国的越南政策。

在其漫长的一生中,罗素完成了 40 余部著作,涉及哲学、数学、伦理学、社会学、教育、历史、宗教以及政治等各个方面。他的首要事业和建树是在数学和逻辑学领域,对西方的哲学产生了深刻影响。中年时期所写的有关道德、政治、教育及和平主义等方面的论述,激励和启发了富于进取精神的人。晚年在积极反对制造核武器和反对越南战争的斗争中,鼓舞了全世界有理想的青年。

罗素著有《数学原理》(*The Principles of Mathematics*,1903)、《意义与真理的研究》(*An Inquiry into Meaning and Truth*,1940)、《人类知识的范围及其限度》(*Human Knowledge: Its Scope and Limits*,1948)、《物的分析》(*The Analysis of Matter*,1927)以及《心的分析》(*The Analysis of Mind*,1921)等著作。写了数十篇散文,其中有《自由人的崇拜》(*The Free Man's Worship*)、《为什么要打仗》(*Why Men Fight*)、《我为何写作》(*Why I Write*)以及《中国问题》(*The Problem of*

China)等散文佳作。他的散文节奏感明显、哲理性强、语言简洁、朴实无华。

散文《怎样步入老年》(*How to Grow Old*)是罗素哲学生涯的结晶。他善意地向读者提出忠告:正确对待人生,不虚度晚年,超越自我,把自己溶合于宇宙万物之中。本篇散文文笔流畅、文字精湛、风格娴熟。文中充满机智幽默、趣文轶事和独特的"似非而是"(paradox)的修辞手法,使之成为脍炙人口的佳作。

三、小说阅读

原文:

The Last Leaf

O. Henry

Many artists lived in the Greenwich Village area of New York. Two young women named Sue and Johnsy shared a studio apartment at the top of a three-story building. Johnsy's real name was Joanna.

In November, a cold, unseen stranger came to visit the city. This disease, pneumonia, killed many people. Johnsy lay on her bed, hardly moving. She looked through the small window. She could see the side of the brick house next to her building.

One morning, a doctor examined Johnsy and took her temperature. Then he spoke with Sue in another room.

"She has one chance in—let us say ten," he said. "And that chance is for her to want to live. Your friend has made up her mind that she is not going to get well. Has she anything on her mind?"

"She, she wanted to paint the Bay of Naples in Italy some day," said Sue.

"Paint?" said the doctor. "Bosh! Has she anything on her mind worth thinking twice—a man for example?"

"A man?" said Sue. "Is a man worth—but, no, doctor; there is nothing of the kind."

"I will do all that science can do," said the doctor. "But whenever my patient begins to count the carriages at her funeral, I take away fifty percent from the curative power of medicines."

After the doctor had gone, Sue went into the workroom and cried. Then she went to Johnsy's room with her drawing board, whistling ragtime.

Johnsy lay with her face toward the window. Sue stopped whistling, thinking she was asleep. She began making a pen and ink drawing for a story in a magazine. Young artists must work their way to "Art" by making pictures for magazine stories. Sue heard a low sound, several times repeated. She went quickly to the bedside.

Johnsy's eyes were open wide. She was looking out the window and counting—counting backward. "Twelve," she said, and a little later "eleven"; and then "ten" and "nine"; and then "eight" and "seven", almost together.

Sue looked out the window. What was there to count? There was only an empty yard and the blank side of the house seven meters away. An old ivy vine, going bad at the roots, climbed half way up the wall. The cold breath of autumn had stricken leaves from the plant until its branches, almost bare, hung on the bricks.

"What is it, dear?" asked Sue.

"Six," said Johnsy, quietly. "They're falling faster now. Three days ago there were almost a hundred. It made my head hurt to count them. But now it's easy. There goes another one. There are only five left now."

"Five what, dear?" asked Sue.

"Leaves. On the plant. When the last one falls I must go, too. I've known that for three days. Didn't the doctor tell you?"

"Oh, I never heard of such a thing," said Sue. "What have old ivy leaves to do with your getting well? And you used to love that vine. Don't be silly. Why, the doctor told me this morning that your chances for getting well real soon were—let's see exactly what he said—he said the chances were ten to one! Try to eat some soup now. And, let me go back to my drawing, so I can sell it to the magazine and buy food and wine for us."

"You needn't get any more wine," said Johnsy, keeping her eyes fixed out the window. "There goes another one. No, I don't want any soup. That leaves just four. I want to see the last one fall before it gets dark. Then I'll go, too."

"Johnsy, dear," said Sue, "will you promise me to keep your eyes closed, and not look out the window until I am done working? I must hand those drawings in by tomorrow."

"Tell me as soon as you have finished," said Johnsy, closing her eyes and lying white and still as a fallen statue. "I want to see the last one fall. I'm tired of waiting. I'm tired of thinking. I want to turn loose my hold on everything, and go sailing down, down, just like one of those poor, tired leaves."

"Try to sleep," said Sue. "I must call Mister Behrman up to be my model for my drawing of an old miner. Don't try to move until I come back."

Old Behrman was a painter who lived on the ground floor of the apartment building. Behrman was a failure in art. For years, he had always been planning to paint a work of art, but had never yet begun it. He earned a little money by serving as a model to artists who could not pay for a professional model. He was a fierce, little, old man who protected the two young women in the studio apartment above him.

Sue found Behrman in his room. In one area was a blank canvas that had been waiting twenty-five years for the first line of paint. Sue told him about Johnsy and how she feared that her friend would float away like a leaf.

Old Behrman was angered at such an idea. "Are there people in the world with the foolishness to die because leaves drop off a vine? Why do you let that silly business come in her brain?"

"She is very sick and weak," said Sue, "and the disease has left her mind full of strange ideas."

"This is not any place in which one so good as Miss Johnsy shall lie sick," yelled Behrman. "Some day I will paint a masterpiece, and we shall all go away."

Johnsy was sleeping when they went upstairs. Sue pulled the shade down to cover the window. She and Behrman went into the other room. They looked out a window fearfully at the ivy vine. Then they looked at each other without speaking. A cold rain was falling, mixed with snow. Behrman sat and posed as the miner.

The next morning, Sue awoke after an hour's sleep. She found Johnsy with wide-open eyes staring at the covered window.

"Pull up the shade; I want to see," she ordered, quietly. Sue obeyed.

After the beating rain and fierce wind that blew through the night, there yet stood against the wall one ivy leaf. It was the last one on the vine. It was still dark green at the center. But its edges were colored with the yellow. It hung bravely from the branch about seven meters above the ground.

"It is the last one," said Johnsy. "I thought it would surely fall during the night. I heard the wind. It will fall today and I shall die at the same time."

"Dear, dear!" said Sue, leaning her worn face down toward the bed. "Think of me, if you won't think of yourself. What would I do?"

But Johnsy did not answer.

The next morning, when it was light, Johnsy demanded that the window shade be raised. The ivy leaf was still there. Johnsy lay for a long time, looking at it. And then she called to Sue, who was preparing chicken soup.

"I've been a bad girl," said Johnsy. "Something has made that last leaf stay there to show me how bad I was. It is wrong to want to die. You may bring me a little soup now."

An hour later she said, "Someday I hope to paint the Bay of Naples."

Later in the day, the doctor came, and Sue talked to him in the hallway.

"Even chances," said the doctor. "With good care, you'll win. And now I must see another case I have in your building. Behrman, his name is—some kind of an artist, I believe. Pneumonia, too. He is an old, weak

第六章　英语阅读教学经典研读实践探索

man and his case is severe. There is no hope for him; but he goes to the hospital today to ease his pain."

The next day, the doctor said to Sue: "She's out of danger. You won. Nutrition and care now—that's all."

Later that day, Sue came to the bed where Johnsy lay, and put one arm around her.

"I have something to tell you, white mouse," she said. "Mister Behrman died of pneumonia today in the hospital. He was sick only two days. They found him the morning of the first day in his room downstairs helpless with pain. His shoes and clothing were completely wet and icy cold. They could not imagine where he had been on such a terrible night."

"And then they found a lantern, still lighted. And they found a ladder that had been moved from its place. And art supplies and a painting board with green and yellow colors mixed on it."

"And look out the window, dear, at the last ivy leaf on the wall. Didn't you wonder why it never moved when the wind blew? Ah, darling, it is Behrman's masterpiece—he painted it there the night that the last leaf fell."

(This story was adapted by Shelley Gollust.)

译文：
最后一片叶子

许多画家居住在纽约的格林威治村。两名年轻女子，休易和乔安西在一栋三层楼的楼顶上，共用一个工作室。乔安西的真名叫乔安娜。

到了11月，一位冷酷、看不见的不速之客闯进了这座城市，这位客人就是肺炎，很多人因它丧了命。乔安西躺在床上没有力气动弹，两眼呆望着小窗，只能看到靠近她这座楼的一座砖房的外墙。

一天上午，医生为乔安西做了检查，为她量了体温，把休易叫到旁边的屋子里。

"现在十成希望只剩下一成。"医生说，"这一成希望取决于她抱不抱活下去的决心。你的这位朋友已经认定自己再也好不了。就不知她还有什么心事吗？"

"她希望有一天能去画那不勒斯湾。"休易答道。

"画画？你扯到哪儿去啦！我是问她心里有没有还留恋的事。比方说,心里还会想着哪位男人?"

"男人?"休易说,"男人还会值得——但是,没有,医生:没这种事。"

"我一定尽力而为,凡医学上有的办法都会采用。"医生说,"但是如果病人盘算起会有多少辆马车送葬来,药物的疗效就要打个对折。"

医生走了以后,休易到画室里哭了一场。哭过后她拿着画板昂首阔步走进乔安西的房间,还一边吹口哨。

乔安西脸朝窗躺着。休易以为她睡着了,忙不吹了。她摆好画板,开始替杂志社作小说的画笔通插图。年轻的美术工作者要闯出艺术之路得先替杂志社作小说的插图。她听到一个低低的声音,并且重复了多次。她迅速走到床边。

乔安西睁大着眼在望窗外,数着数——是倒着数的。"十二",她数着,过了一会儿,"十一"。又过了会儿,"十""九"。又过了会儿,"八""七",两个数几乎是接着数出来的。

休易看着窗外。有什么可数呢？见到的只是个空荡荡的冷落院子和七米外一栋砖房的墙。一根老藤趴在墙上,有半堵墙高,靠近根部的地方已经萎缩,藤叶几乎全被冷飕飕的秋风吹落,只剩下光秃秃的枝干还紧贴在破败的墙上。

"怎么啦,亲爱的?"休易问。

"六,"乔安西的声音低得几乎听不见,"现在落得快了。三天前还有将近一百,叫我数得头发痛。现在容易。又掉了一片,只剩下五片。"

"五片什么,亲爱的?"休易问。

"藤叶。那根藤上的。等最后一片掉下来,我也就完了。早三天我已经明白。难道医生没对你说?"

"天哪,我从来没有听说过这种说法,"休易说,"一根老藤上的叶子跟你的病好转有什么相干？你一向很喜欢那根葡萄藤的。不要这么傻里傻气。今天上午医生还对我说,你很快好起来的希望是——让我想想他的原话来着——对啦,他说你的希望有九成！快喝点儿汤吧,喝了我就再画画,卖给杂志,得了钱买葡萄酒,再买点吃的。"

"葡萄酒用不着再买,"乔安西说,眼睛还盯着窗外,"又掉了一片。汤我也不要。只剩下四片叶了。要是天黑前我看到最后一片掉下来就好,见到了我也好闭眼。"

第六章 英语阅读教学经典研读实践探索

"乔安西,亲爱的,"休易说,"你答应我。闭上眼睛,别再看窗外,等我把这幅插图画完,怎么样?这些画明天等着交。"

"那你画完了得告诉我。"乔安西边说边闭上眼睛,脸惨白,躺着不动,像尊倒下的石膏像,"我想要看最后一片落下,我不愿再等。也不愿想什么。一切我都不要了,只愿像一片没有了生命力的败叶一样,往下飘,飘。"

"你争取睡一会儿,"休易说,"我画老矿工要个模特儿,得找贝尔曼来。我只出去一会儿。别动,等我回来。"

贝尔曼老头也能画画,就住在下面一楼,贝尔曼在艺术上并不成功。他一心要画出个惊人之作,但至今还没开笔。近些年他就靠给这一带请不起职业模特儿的年轻画家当模特儿挣几个钱。这小个子老头像个凶神恶煞,自诩保护楼上两位年轻的画家。

休易去时,贝尔曼果然在房间,屋角里有一块白画布,就等画上幅惊人之作,但等了二十五年还是一笔未画。休易告诉了他关于乔安西的事情,她的朋友将像叶子一样飘走。

贝尔曼老头听到这般想法很生气:"看到葡萄藤叶子掉了就会想死,世界上还真有这种傻子?你怎么让那种怪事钻到她脑瓜子里去啦?"

"她病得厉害,身体太虚弱,"休易说,"脑子烧糊涂了,老胡思乱想。"

"乔安西小姐是大好人,怎么就病倒在这种地方?"贝尔曼吼道,"哪天我画出张绝妙的画,我们一块儿远走高飞。"

两人上楼时乔安西睡着了。休易把窗帘放得严严实实,她和贝尔曼走进另一间房。他们在房里瞧着窗外的那根藤,心里不由得害怕。接着,两人你看我,我看你,好一会儿没说话。

冰冷的雨在不停地下,还夹着雪。贝尔曼坐下来,扮作一名矿工。

休易只睡了一个小时,到早上醒来时,只见乔安西睁大眼睛盯着被挡住的窗户。

"卷起来,我要看。"她有气无力地说。休易照办了。

经过漫漫长夜的风吹雨打,竟然还有一片藤叶扒在砖墙上。这是藤上的最后一片叶,叶子中间依旧是深绿,但边缘已经发黄。它顽强地挂在离地面七米高的一根枝上。

"这是最后一片叶,"乔安西说,"我还以为晚上它准会掉。我听见了风声。今天它会掉的,我的死期也就来了。"

"乖乖,乖乖!"休易说,把憔悴的脸扭到床的另一侧,"你不愿为自己着想也得为我着想。丢下我怎么办呢?"

但是乔安西没有答话。

第二天天刚亮,乔安西又吩咐把窗帘拉上去。藤叶还在。乔安西躺在床上久久看着。后来她唤休易,休易正在做鸡汤。

乔安西说:"休易,我太不应该。不知是怎么鬼使神差的,那片叶老掉不下来,可见我原来心绪不好。想死是罪过。你这就给我盛点鸡汤来!"

过了一小时,她说:"休易,我希望以后能去画那不勒斯湾。"

下午医生来了。休易在走廊问起医生。

"有五成希望。"医生说,"只要护理得好,就能战胜疾病。现在我得去楼下看另一个人。他叫贝尔曼——肯定也是个画画的。又是肺炎。他年纪大,体质弱,病又来势凶,已经没有了希望,但今天还是要送医院,让他舒服些。"

第二天,医生对休易说:"她出了危险期。你们胜利了。剩下的事是营养和护理。"

这天下午,休易坐到乔交西躺的床上.她伸出只胳膊提着乔安西。

"有件事告诉你,小宝贝,"她说,"贝尔曼先生得肺炎今天死在医院。他只病了两天。头一天早上人们在楼下房间发现他难受得要命,鞋子、衣服全湿了,摸起来冰凉。谁也猜不着他在又是风又是雨的夜晚上哪儿去了。后来他们发现了一盏灯笼,还亮着,又发现梯子搬动了地方,还有一些画画用的东西,一块调色板,上面调了绿颜料和黄颜料。现在你看窗外,乖乖。墙上还扒着最后一片藤叶。你不是奇怪为什么风吹着它也不飘不动吗?唉,亲爱的,那是贝尔曼的杰作——在最后一片叶子落下来的晚上,他在墙上画了一片。"

(注:本篇故事由雪莱·高尔斯特改编。)

作者简介及作品欣赏:

欧·亨利(O. Henry,1862—1910)是威廉·西德尼·波特(William Sydney Porter)的笔名,美国著名作家。他出生于美国北卡罗来纳州,早年在北卡罗来纳和德克萨斯州生活,曾做过牧场帮工和银行职员。他30岁时成为一名记者,并开始创作短篇小说。

欧·亨利是一位多产作家,一生创作过250部短篇小说。他的主要作品有短篇小说集《白菜和国王》(Cabbages and Kings,1904),《饰边台灯》(*The Trimmed Lamp*,1907),《命运之路》(*Roads of Destiny*,1909)和《乱七八糟》(*Sixes and Sevens*,1911)等。他的短篇小说以广大的城市贫民百姓为对象,反映了他们的现实生活。欧·亨利在他的作品中提倡穷人与富人应受到同样的尊敬与重视。因此,他的作品受到大众的欢迎。此外,他注重小说情节描写,故事发展的节奏较快,充满幽默与活力,结尾往往出人意外,含意深远,给人以耳目一新的感觉。

《最后一片叶子》(*The Last Leaf*)描述了一名画家为了激励另一位重病的画家鼓起生的勇气,冒着寒风为她描画最后一片绿叶,最后自己受寒,死于肺炎。这篇小说内容感人至深,结局出人意料,是欧·亨利文学创作手法的典型代表作。

第三节 名言警句阅读与欣赏

Keep your eyes on the stars and your feet on the ground.
展望星空,脚踏实地。(展望未来,立足现在。)
Knowledge is power.
知识就是力量。
Hope for the best and prepare for the worst!
做最坏的打算,期盼最好的结果。(做好两手准备。)
Great minds think alike.
英雄所见略同。(智者同思。)
If you think you can, you can.
你想你能,你就能。
To the world, you may be one person, but to one person, you may be the world.
对于世界,你是一个人;对于一个人,你是整个世界。(大你和小你。)
Luck is when preparation meets opportunity.
运气就是有备遇到机会。(运气偏爱于有准备之人。)
Perhaps luck exists somewhere between the world of planning and the world of chance.

也许运气存在于运筹和机会之间。(计划人生,机会多多,幸运之所在。)

A foreign language is a weapon in the struggle of life. (Karl Marx)

外国语是人生斗争的武器。(卡尔·马克思)

己所不欲,勿施于人。(孔子)

译文 1:Do unto others as thou would have them do unto thee. (Confucius)

(按文体的一致性,古汉语对应于古英语,这种翻译算是对应的双语的意、体和格。)

译文 2:Do not do to others what you don't want to be done to you. (Confucius)

(按现代英语的通俗表达法,改译为现代英语,谓之"古为今用""中为洋用"。)

有教无类。(孔子)

Education for all. (Confucius)

第四节 独立阅读实践训练

Passage 1

Immigration into Britain

David Goodhart dislikes immigration. He thinks Britain has made a colossal mistake by being so open to foreigners over the years. The efforts of the current Conservative-led coalition government to drastically reduce net immigration do not, in his view, go far enough. He not only disapproves of ghettoes, where immigrants subsist on welfare and fail to integrate into British society. He also dislikes places like London's financial district and Silicon Valley, with their highly productive, English-speaking immigrants. He can just about tolerate foreign players in the English Premier League, but that is about it.

He has many reasons. New arrivals make life harder for native workers, asserts Mr. Goodhart, who runs Demos, a centre-left thinktank. They compete for public services. Their ghettoes are an affront to common decency. By making Britain more diverse, they have reduced fellow feeling. When a country has lots of immigrants, its residents turn against the welfare state: people are less inclined to contribute money to a system that seems to benefit people who do not look like them. The churn of new arrivals also makes it harder to integrate previous generations of immigrants.

So runs Mr. Goodhart's argument. His position is not original, although he has made the argument about immigration undermining the welfare state his own. Nearly all British people agree with him that there is far too much immigration. But *The British Dream* is not consistently polemical. Wrapped in an insistent, occasionally intemperate argument about the malign effects of immigration is something much more interesting: an analysis of how immigrants have fared in Britain, and how they have changed the country. This bit of the book (roughly the middle 250 pages) is fairly unbiased, well-researched and shrewd—so much so that it makes Mr. Goodhart's conclusions seem rather odd.

The immigrant Britain described in this book is hugely diverse—almost as much so as British society itself. There are, the author explains, enormous differences between west African and east African immigrants, between Pakistanis from the Mirpur Valley and Pakistanis from Lahore. Afro-Caribbean women fare much better than Afro-Caribbean men. Some groups, like the Indians kicked out of Uganda by Idi Amin, have succeeded spectacularly. Others, like Somalis, are in desperate shape. Some, like Indians, are economically integrated but still tend to marry among themselves; for others, like Afro-Caribbeans, the reverse is true. And everybody is becoming more mixed.

(一)词汇

ghetto	n.	犹太人区,贫民窟
subsist on		以……为生;靠……生存
centre-left	adj.	左派的
affront	n.	公开侮辱,轻蔑
churn	n.	搅乳器;人事变更率
polemical	adj.	好争辩的
intemperate	adj.	放纵的
malign	adj.	恶毒的
fare	vi.	遭遇,进展,过活
unbiased	adj.	没有偏见的,公正的

(二)长难句

(1) ...people are less inclined to contribute money to a system that seems to benefit people who do not look like them.

他们可不愿意为这个制度花钱,如果受益的将是外来人。

分析:句子主干为"People are less inclined.",主语为people,系动词为are,表语为less inclined,to contribute money to a system that seems to benefit people who do not look like them是表语补足语。that seems to benefit people who do not look like them是定语从句修饰a system。

(2) Wrapped in an insistent, occasionally intemperate argument about the malign effects of immigration is something much more interesting: an analysis of how immigrants have fared in Britain, and how they have changed the country.

置身于强悍的辩论之下,书中还是不乏一些有意思的成分:不仅分析了移民在这里取得成功的方式,还分析了移民是怎样改变英国社会的。

分析：句子主干为"Argument is something more interesting."，主语为 argument，系动词是 is，表语为 something more interesting。wrapped in an insistent 是省略结构，补充完整是 although the argument was wrapped in an insistent。an analysis of how immigrants have fared in Britain, and how they have changed the country 是 something much more interesting 的同位语。how they have changed the country 补充完整是 an analysis of how they have changed the country。

(3) The immigrant Britain described in this book is hugely diverse—almost as much so as British society itself.

书中的移民也是各具特色——几乎不亚于真正的英国社会。

分析：句子主干是"The immigrant Britain is hugely diverse."，主语为 the immigrant Britain，系动词为 is，表语为 diverse。described in this book 是后置定语修饰主语，hugely 是程度副词作状语，almost as much so as British society itself 也是表示程度的状语，在这里是对 hugely diverse 的进一步说明。

(三) 参考译文

移民英国

David Goodhart 讨厌外来移民。他认为英国犯了一个天大的错误，这些年来不应该对外国人这么开放。虽然如今保守党领导的联合政府加大力度大量削减净移民人数，但是 David 觉得这还远远不够。他不仅讨厌贫民窟，在这里移民靠救济金度日而且没法融入英国社会；他还讨厌伦敦金融区和硅谷，这里有不少讲一口流利英语的高产移民。他能接受的也就是英超联赛的外籍球员，这已经是他所能接受的极限了。

他之所以持这样的态度理由多的是。他说外来人口使得本国人民生活更加艰难，他本人目前经营了一个叫 Demos 的左派智囊团。移民和当地人竞争公共资源，他们的住所影响市容。他们一方面使得英国更加多元化，另一方面也减少了英国人的同情心。一个国家移民多了，当地人就会变得开始反对福利国家：他们可不愿意为这个制度花钱，如果受益的将是外来人。不仅如此，新来者的更迭使得要整合上一代移民变得更加困难。

Goodhart 的论调大抵如此。虽然他提出了所谓移民将有损福利国家的理论,但其观点仍不算新颖。大多数英国人对于他的"外来人爆棚"一说都持赞同态度。然而《英国梦》也不是一本始终忙于争辩的书。置身于强悍的辩论之下,书中还是不乏一些有意思的成分:不仅分析了移民在这里取得成功的方式,还分析了移民是怎样改变英国社会的。这一部分(大约 250 页)还是相当中肯公正的,其证据确凿,论述精确,也许是因为作者太过精明反而得出了一个奇怪的结论。

书中的移民也是各具特色——几乎不亚于真正的英国社会。作者说,西非和东非移民之间,来自 Mirpur 谷和来自 Lahore 的巴基斯坦人之间,本身就有很多差异。在非裔加勒比人中,女性比男性生活得要好。其他种族的英国移民也吃尽了苦头。印度人在经济上已经与世界接轨,却仍然倾向于与同族人婚配,他们的这一点刚好跟非裔加勒比人相反。但无论怎样,大家的融合度已经变得越来越高了。

Passage 2

A paralysed woman gets herself a drink

Helping yourself to a cup of coffee may seem like a small, everyday thing. But not if you are quadriplegic. Unlike paraplegics, for whom the robotic legs described in the previous article are being developed, quadriplegics have lost the use of all four limbs. Yet thanks to a project organised by John Donoghue of Brown University, in Rhode Island, and his colleagues, they too have hope. One of the participants in his experiments, a 58-year-old woman who is unable to use any of her limbs, can now pick up a bottle containing coffee and bring it close enough to her mouth to drink from it using a straw. She does so using a thought-controlled robotic arm fixed to a nearby stand. It is the first time she has managed something like that since she suffered a stroke, nearly 15 years ago.

Arms are more complicated pieces of machinery than legs, so controlling them via electrodes attached to the skin of someone's scalp is not yet possible. Instead, brain activity has to be recorded directly. And that is what Dr. Donoghue is doing. Both his female participant and a second individual, a man of 66 also paralysed by a stroke, have worked with him before, as a result of which they have had small, multichannel electrodes implanted in the parts of the motor cortexes of their brains associated with hand movements. The woman's implant was put there in 2005; the man's five months before the latest trial, described in a paper just published in *Nature*.

Dr. Donoghue and his team decoded signals from their participants' brains as they were asked to imagine controlling a robotic arm making preset movements. The volunteers were then encouraged to operate one of two robot arms by thinking about the movements they wanted to happen. When the software controlling the arms detected the relevant signals, the arms moved appropriately.

The arm that the woman used to help herself to a drink is a lightweight device developed by DLR, Germany's Aerospace Centre, as part of its robotics programme. The other, known as a DEKA arm, is being developed in America specifically as a prosthetic for those who have lost an arm. Normally, it is operated by the wearer moving his chest or moving his toes over buttons in a shoe. The participants used it to reach and grasp a ball made of foam rubber.

（一）词汇

paraplegic	n.	截瘫病人
robotic	adj.	机器人的，机械的
quadriplegic	n.	四肢瘫痪者
limb	n.	肢，腿
straw	n.	吸管，稻草
scalp	n.	头皮
paralyse	vt.	使瘫痪，使麻痹
stroke	n.	中风
electrode	n.	电极
preset	adj.	预置的
prosthetic	n.	假肢

(二)长难句

(1) One of the participants in his experiments, a 58-year-old woman who is unable to use any of her limbs, can now pick up a bottle containing coffee and bring it close enough to her mouth to drink from it using a straw.

一名58岁的四肢瘫痪女患者作为实验的被试,现在已经可以自行拿起一杯咖啡并且送到嘴边用吸管饮用,而在此之前她是完全无法支配四肢的。

分析:句子主干为"One of the participants can pick up a bottle and bring it.",主语为 one of the participants,第一个谓语为 can pick up,其宾语为 a bottle,第二个谓语为(can)bring,其宾语为 it。in his experiments 作定语,a 58-year-old woman,who is unable to use any of her limbs 作主语的同位语,和主语指代相同的对象,其中 who 引导一个定语从句,containing 是 V-ing 的非谓语形式,因为 contain 是 bottle 发出的动作,所以用-ing 形式表示主动发出,这里可以理解为 which contains coffee,to drink from it 是动词不定式的主动形式表示被动意义,using a straw 前面省略了 by,表示方式。

(2) Both his female participant and a second individual, a man of 66 also paralysed by a stroke, have worked with him before, as a result of which they have had small, multichannel electrodes implanted in the parts of the motor cortexes of their brains associated with hand movements.

他的这位女性被试和一名66岁同样因中风而瘫痪的男性被试,因为两人之前都曾与他一起共事过,所以在他们控制手掌运动的大脑运动皮质中都被植入了一些小型多通道的电极。

分析:主句句子主干为"His female participant and a second individual have worked.",主语为 his female participant and a second individual,谓语为 have worked,with him before 为状语。as a result of 后接一个结果状语从句,其主干为"They have had electrodes implanted.",主语为 they,谓语为 have had … implanted,宾语为 electrodes。in the parts of the motor cortexes of their brains associated with hand movements 作地点状语,其中 associated 前面省略了 which are。

(三)参考译文

瘫痪女性也能自助喝水

除非你是位四肢瘫痪的病人,否则靠自己的力气喝上一杯咖啡怎么看都是一件再容易不过的日常小事。和截瘫患者不同,正如上一篇文章所说的那样,能够帮助截瘫患者的机械腿正在研发当中,而四肢瘫痪者的四肢完全不能正常工作。得益于罗德岛布朗大学的 John Donoghue 博士和他的同事们正在研究的一个项目,四肢瘫痪患者也看到了希望。一名58岁的四肢瘫痪女患者作为实验的被试,现在已经可以自行拿起一杯咖啡并且送到嘴边用吸管饮用,而在此之前她是完全无法支配四肢的。实验的成功是借助于一个固定在她身边的机械手臂,此手臂由思维控制。这也是在她因中风瘫痪了15年后第一次做成这一类事。

相对于腿而言,手臂的机械属性更加复杂,所以目前要通过头皮上的电极来实现控制手臂的条件尚未成熟。另一方面,大脑活动只能被直接记录。这也是 Donoghue 博士目前的研究内容。他的这位女性被试和一名66岁同样因中风而瘫痪的男性被试,因为两人之前都曾与他一起共事过,所以在他们控制手掌运动的大脑运动皮质中都被植入了一些小型多通道的电极。根据最近《自然》杂志发表的一篇文章,女性被试的电极植入于2005年,而男性被试的电极在最近一次实验的5个月前被植入。

当被试按要求来设想控制一个机器手臂完成预计动作时,Donoghue 博士和他的团队从被试的大脑里解码出信号。接着实验员鼓励被试通过想象后者需要的动作来操作两种机器人手臂中的一种。当软件控制机械手臂侦测到相关信号时,手臂就能相应地移动。

女性被试用来辅助自己喝水的轻量装置由德国宇航中心研发制成,是其机器人技术项目的一部分。另一种称为 DEKA 的手臂,是美国专门为断臂人研发的假肢。常态下,佩戴者通过胸部动作或是在鞋里面的按键上移动脚趾来进行操作。被试用它来触摸并抓握泡沫橡胶球。

参考文献

[1]沙夫津.兰登书屋:英语智慧阅读一周通[M].卢丹,朴玉,谢亚南,译.长春:长春出版社,2007.

[2]格拉伯,斯托勒.英语阅读教学与研究[M].赵燕,译.天津:天津大学出版社,2020.

[3]格瑞莱特,冯晓媛.英语阅读教学[M].北京:人民教育出版社,2000.

[4]曾亚平.英语阅读与写作研究[M].上海:上海交通大学出版社,2009.

[5]陈葆.英语阅读理解技巧[M].广州:广东高等教育出版社,2005.

[6]陈则航.英语阅读教学与研究[M].北京:外语教学与研究出版社,2016.

[7]崔俊媛.语篇分析与英语阅读教学研究[M].北京:世界图书出版公司,2017.

[8]丁维莉,陈维昌,车竞.篇章理论与英语阅读教学[M].北京:世界图书出版公司,2009.

[9]郭浩儒.大学英语阅读学习方法指导和技能训练[M].北京:宇航出版社,2001.

[10]韩建全,陈晓霞.大学英语阅读[M].成都:西南交通大学出版社,2015.

[11]韩满玲,邓保中.英语阅读的奥秘[M].北京:中国国际广播出版社,2006.

[12]何克胜,张海艳,张娟.初中英语阅读教学对学生核心素养的培养研究[M].长春:吉林人民出版社,2020.

[13]何亚男,应晓球.落实学科核心素养在课堂·高中英语阅读

教学[M].上海:上海教育出版社,2021.

[14]黄远振.英语阅读教学与思维发展[M].南宁:广西教育出版社,2019.

[15]李杰.英语阅读方法学习与能力训练[M].青岛:青岛海洋大学出版社,2001.

[16]李佐文,叶慧君.英语阅读理解策略[M].呼和浩特:内蒙古大学出版社,2005.

[17]刘津开.大学英语阅读策略训练[M].广州:华南理工大学出版社,2006.

[18]吕寅梅.高中英语阅读教学研究与实践[M].北京:光明日报出版社,2019.

[19]马丽娟.聚焦思维品质的高中英语阅读教学[M].长春:吉林人民出版社,2020.

[20]孟留军.大学英语阅读实训[M].合肥:安徽大学出版社,2018.

[21]邵慧.英语阅读教学"中心－框架"模式研究[M].沈阳:东北大学出版社,2020.

[22]佟敏强.大学英语阅读教学理论与实践[M].长春:吉林出版集团有限责任公司,2009.

[23]汪艳萍.英语阅读教学与写作研究[M].北京:世界图书出版公司,2017.

[24]王丹.英语阅读教学理论与实践[M].北京:知识产权出版社,2018.

[25]王笃勤.大学英语阅读教学活动设计[M].哈尔滨:哈尔滨工程大学出版社,2011.

[26]王耿正,曹殿俊,黄付巧.高中英语阅读教学理论应用研究[M].长春:吉林人民出版社,2019.

[27]王婷婷,刘硕,魏纪福.英语阅读与教学研究[M].广州:广东旅游出版社,2018.

[28]文亚光,郑春红.语篇视角下的高中英语阅读教学[M].成都:西南交通大学出版社,2019.

[29]谢丽.大学英语阅读教学理论与实践研究[M].北京:北京理工大学出版社,2015.

[30]游英慧.英语阅读与教学研究[M].北京:光明日报出版

社,2016.

[31]于洋,唐艳.大学英语阅读教学方法研究[M].北京:现代出版社,2019.

[32]张慧芳.英语阅读与教学研究[M].长春:吉林人民出版社,2017.

[33]张湘.主题英语阅读教学的图式交互可视化策略研究[M].广州:广东高等教育出版社,2016.

[34]周荣辉.英语阅读理解策略与技巧[M].成都:西南交通大学出版社,2009.

[35]朱振武.英语阅读范文精华[M].上海:华东理工大学出版社,2020.

[36]庄彩芹.浅谈高中英语阅读教学与研究[M].北京:北京邮电大学出版社,2015.

[37]蔡晗,陈旭光.浅谈英译汉在初中英语阅读教学中的应用[J].校园英语,2022(06):58-60.

[38]蔡丽萍.浅析初中英语阅读教学中的学生思维能力培养[J].校园英语,2022(06):61-63.

[39]曹雪莲.农村中学英语阅读能力培养的策略研究[J].学周刊,2021(33):9-10.

[40]曹宇晖.基于"互联网+"环境下的大学英语阅读教学体系构建研究[J].中国新通信,2022,24(04):189-191.

[41]陈玲玲.思维导图在高中英语阅读教学中的应用研究[J].英语教师,2022,22(03):183-185.

[42]储培.图式理论在中职英语阅读教学的实施对策[J].校园英语,2021(50):53-54.

[43]方阿笋.基于思维品质培养的初中英语阅读教学策略研究[J].校园英语,2022(14):22-24.

[44]葛文庚.新课程背景下高中英语阅读教学策略的调整与优化研究[J].校园英语,2022(13):18-20.

[45]韩琪.新媒体应用于高校英语阅读教学的可行性建议[J].新闻研究导刊,2022,13(08):200-202.

[46]黄悦妍.基于深度学习理念的初中英语阅读教学策略探究[J].校园英语,2022(15):81-83.

[47]焦淑君.核心素养下小学英语阅读教学的实施策略[J].试题与研究,2022(05):107-108.

[48]康月琴.小学英语阅读教学的策略和方法[J].校园英语,2021(49):157-158.

[49]郎睿娟.任务型教学法在职业学院英语阅读教学中的应用[J].科技视界,2022(10):155-157.

[50]李超.现代信息技术与中学英语阅读教学的融合[J].校园英语,2022(08):103-105.

[51]李佳.词块教学法在高中英语阅读教学中的应用研究[J].校园英语,2022(13):30-32.

[52]林仁品."读思言"模式下初中英语阅读教学策略研究[J].英语广场:学术研究,2022(01):125-127.

[53]林燕贞.图式理论在大学英语阅读教学中的应用研究[J].佳木斯职业学院学报,2022,38(05):109-111.

[54]马海香.分层教学法在初中英语阅读教学中的应用[J].学周刊,2022(19):83-85.

[55]糜静燕.基于英语核心素养改进初中英语阅读教学的策略[J].校园英语,2022(08):118-120.

[56]潘蕾.浅析高中英语阅读教学中思维品质的培养方法[J].英语教师,2022,22(04):122-124.

[57]秦金鑫,齐聪.基于图式理论的英语阅读教学研究述评[J].教育观察,2022,11(11):75-78.

[58]商坤.基于批判性思维能力提升的初中英语阅读教学探究[J].英语广场:学术研究,2021(36):131-133.

[59]师丽丹.语块教学法在英语阅读教学中的应用研究[J].河南财政税务高等专科学校学报,2022,36(01):73-76.

[60]宋慧慧.基于思维品质培养的初中英语阅读教学探究[J].英语教师,2022,22(08):168-170.

[61]唐宝凤.高中英语阅读教学中学生思维能力的培养[J].校园英语,2022(06):109-111.

[62]王丹.微课模式下的大学英语阅读教学研究[J].现代英语,2022(06):25-28.

[63]王勤.基于深度学习的初中英语阅读教学策略研究[J].基础

教育论坛(下旬刊),2021(12):74-75.

[64]王玉卓.基于学科核心素养的高中英语阅读教学[J].校园英语,2022(14):112-114.

[65]文慧.高职英语阅读教学中翻转课堂的创新研究[J].山东商业职业技术学院学报,2021,21(06):48-51.

[66]吴靖,许红梅.合作学习应用于英语阅读教学的现实困境及策略探析[J].经济师,2022(04):193-194.

[67]徐玉红.如何把"立德树人"融入小学英语阅读教学中[J].学周刊,2022(04):26-27.

[68]许斌.核心素养理念下的初中英语阅读教学策略探析[J].新课程,2022(06):43.

[69]许祎.新媒体环境下高校英语阅读教学的生态特征及创新模式研究[J].环境工程,2022,40(03):271.

[70]杨九如.课程思政视域下高中英语阅读教学实施路径[J].校园英语,2022(16):54-56.

[71]张国锋.翻转课堂教学模式在初中英语阅读教学中的应用初探[J].新课程,2022(23):162-163.

[72]张莉,杨志皇.基于主题意义的英语阅读教学构思与突破[J].太原城市职业技术学院学报,2022(03):80-82.

[73]张岁太.核心素养下的高中英语阅读教学策略分析[J].科学咨询(教育科研),2022(04):241-243.

[74]张晓丽.初中英语阅读教学中渗透核心素养的有效教学策略[J].考试周刊,2022(14):107-110.

[75]赵俊霞.基于思维导图的高中英语阅读教学应用研究[J].校园英语,2022(01):121-123.

[76]赵秀梅.基于六要素整合活动观的高中英语阅读教学探究[J].甘肃教育研究,2022(04):52-55.

[77]周莉."互联网+"背景下英语阅读教学策略研究[J].高考·上,2022(02):126-128.